MEH
SCAPO
LOGY

How to turn your
"carbon copy"
B2B company into
a growth machine
with differentiation,
positioning, and
un–turn–downable
offers

MATT HODKINSON

MEHscapology

How to turn your "carbon copy" B2B company into a growth machine with differentiation, positioning, and un-turn-downable offers

www.matthodkinson.com

First Edition

Printed in United Kingdom

ISBN: 978-1-3999-4969-9

I. Hodkinson, Matt

Cover design by "Peter & Paul"

Interior design & typesetting by Mario Lampic

Dedication

An immensely practical book that skilfully navigates the reader through a pathway to "mehscape" the "me too" approach to positioning and marketing. Matt balances creativity, fun, science and specificity in a playful way that is guaranteed to create intrigue in any audience.

Keith Howells, Managing Partner at Project 4 Learning Lab

The barrier to entry for consulting firms has all but disappeared over the past decade. In this book, Matt has put together the definitive guide to positioning to win in and amongst a category that's harder than ever for potential prospects to navigate.

Jacob Dutton, Co-Founder & CEO at Future Foundry

MEHscapology highlights all the key areas where businesses (including us), feel like they have hit that grey area of the "same old, same old" approach to marketing and positioning. The book remains engaging and comical in parts. The content's easy to follow, contains great guidance, and Matt's refreshed approach to marketing. Overall the book is one that can be read all at once and then picked up along the way, or to be used as a planned step by step approach.

Stephanie Parker, Client Services Manager at Singularitee

Mehscapology is the book you all need to read this year. Matt's knowledge of the subject is undeniable. His guidance is what every marketer needs, and he presents the facts clearly and concisely. If you read this book and follow his step-by-step advice, you will no longer fall into the 'Meh' trap.

Ailish O'Dowd, Marketing Director at The Project Foundry

If you're looking for a practical and insightful guide to help your brand stand out in today's crowded marketplace, look no further. MEHscapology will jolt you out of your comfort zone and position your business in your own unique category, from which every client conversation and opportunity will flow. This book is a game-changer for anyone looking to differentiate their brand and rise above the competition.

Tony Clark, Founder & CEO at NextWave

Matt's experience, humour and expertise shine through in MEHscapology. It provides easily digestible and practical advice for your business positioning, as well as finding your route to success. We work with so many businesses that need a greater focus on differentiation, and will definitely be spreading the word!

Peter Czapp, Co-Founder at The Wow Company

TABLE OF CONTENTS

A MEHxplanation

The word MEH has become common parlance in recent times to describe anything that results in an underwhelming or apathetic response. MEH first entered my consciousness in my last business, Influence Agents. As a professional marketer (itself such a generic label), I felt the crushing weight of expectation to be one step ahead of competitors in an incredibly crowded sector.

I found it difficult to shake the feeling that, were potential clients to hold us under any sort of spotlight or due diligence, they'd find us to be just like any other marketing agency on offer. We had very little, if any, differentiation and our website copy, emails and sales pitch all took inspiration from others in the sector, following the advice of those firmly indoctrinated in the "path well-trodden". As a result, we were saying nothing new: looking and sounding like any other agency in the marketplace.

In short, we were very MEH!

When it's literally your job to help others to stand out and be noticed by the right people, it feels pretty fraudulent not to be able to demonstrate the same for yourself.

Call it a case of "the cobbler's kids" (the proverb says that they're the ones with "no shoes", in the ultimate demonstration of irony) or "imposter syndrome". Whatever it was, I was custodian of a somewhat dull, run-of-the-mill business, generating the sort of mediocre results and limited growth it deserved.

We'd often lose out to competitors that themselves weren't positioned particularly well. With stagnant growth, a handful of clients that we tolerated more than enjoyed working with and the constant frustration at swinging and missing at the goals we'd set for ourselves and the business, it became clear that something had to change.

At this point, I still hadn't diagnosed the problem. I investigated further, delving into our CRM system in an attempt to recognise any themes and trends in the data. Why was it that we couldn't break through this growth ceiling? Why had we consistently failed to generate the attention we so desperately craved? And why had we so often lost out to "lesser" agencies?

There were times when we suffered from the feast-and-famine rollercoaster that befalls many small businesses that must juggle marketing and delivery. We'd put a heavy emphasis on promotional activity for a while; it would work (to an extent) and bring in a glut of new clients, who then rightfully commanded our attention and needed serving to the highest level possible.

And that inevitably meant taking our eye off the marketing side of things. Of course, what followed was a very dry pipeline while we focused on client delivery. By the time we needed to onboard new clients, to replace those we were completing our work with, there were no prospects to convert.

You've heard this story before and maybe even encountered it yourself. Perhaps it was even the reason that prompted you to acquire this book!

The truth is that our mere presence in the market should have attracted more inbound attention and enquiries than it did. So why did our messaging and pipeline generation only really serve us when we gave it our full attention?

> *I finally unearthed the stark evidence that I'd unwittingly built a "carbon copy" business: one with no discernible differentiating factors from others in the industry.*

Prospects that did encounter our website, emails, social posts and other marketing activities were less than excited by what they found.

We were seen as "just another marketing agency", rather than people they'd be genuinely excited to work with (the type of response that we elicit nowadays, I'm glad to say!).

It was at this point that I resolved to do something about our unavoidably MEH position in the market.

In researching the underlying causes of MEH and the component parts of an un-pigeon-holeable market position, I learned that it's less about creativity and marketing nous and much more about understanding the "Buyer Brain". That is, the psychological reasoning that informs any considered purchase decision and, more simply, the specific elements that anyone must know or feel before they will even pay attention to you, let alone buy anything.

It's not the wholly creative, arts-and-crafty style of marketing that many would have you believe. I've learned that great marketing is as much about the constants as it is about the creative process. There are, in fact, many hard-and-fast factors that have remained unchanged since the hunter-gathering days of humanity.

In short, there are metaphorical checkboxes in the buyer brain that your positioning and messaging must tick to unlock the potential of any marketing channel. This will leave you as the only viable option for your buyers to end their pain, solve their challenge and realise their true potential – whatever specialist area you occupy.

In this book, I reveal those component parts and checkboxes, as well as the overall structure for a competition-free B2B offer.

When you're done with this process, you'll possess a superior offer and an incomparable market position to anyone in your industry. When you apply and "activate" the offer (I'll show you how), you'll attract the attention of your ideal buyer and retain that attention throughout the sales conversation.

I can't wait to hear all about the results you generate after completing this completely painless transformation!

What does MEHscapology look like?

On the face of it, MEHscapology is made up of three key areas:

Full differentiation: the ability to claim with clarity and confidence to be the "world's only…" in your specific and unique area of specialism.

Ownership of **an un-turn-downable offer**: the ability to compel buyers with your message, to account for their many requirements throughout the buyer journey and to invalidate all alternatives with ease, switching your prospect off the idea of taking any competing path.

A targeted and highly-personalised approach to reaching your target audience: a malleable enough position to be able to tailor for the buyer who sits before you without the need to niche your entire business (a sure-fire way to expose yourself to unnecessary risk).

There's more.

Whilst this book speaks to the need to escape MEH in the positioning and marketing sense, you may be feeling MEH about various other aspects of your business:

A MEH sales pipeline or growth trajectory: one that falls short of the goals and expectations you've set for your company. Perhaps you consistently fall short of the goals you set for revenue and other key metrics, however realistic they may be. The intention is there but when reality bites, it bites hard.

A MEH company culture or level of employee satisfaction. It can be tricky to balance success on the books with a happy and healthy workplace. Often, we sacrifice attention to office culture and enjoyment, as well as our physical and mental health, in order to satisfy the client. Nobody intends for this to happen but much like the "death by a thousand cuts", we allow small things to build, until the "new norm" becomes something that we no longer recognise as our own and find near-impossible to reverse.

A MEH operational setup: impacting client retention and project success rates. This often results from favouring the "getting the job done" approach rather than building repeatable and effective processes for delivery as we go. Before we know it, clients are receiving very different experiences from one another and your ability to deliver success is compromised.

Full MEHscapology would mean eradicating any sense of apathy, discomfort or dissatisfaction in the way that you run your business and the results that you generate for yourself and your staff.

But it doesn't stop there.

A well-run business can be a vehicle to a better personal life. Many entrepreneurs founded their business on the promise of more freedom and wealth, creating opportunity and the ability to unlock new experiences for themselves and their families. So, true MEHscapology would also allow you to remove any perceived shortcomings in your home life as well as at work.

No small task.

In these pages, I'll focus on fixing any shortcomings in your ability to position and market your solutions and products. But my most sincere wish is that this sets you on a path to full MEHscapology in all aspects of life and sets your expectations and ambitions higher than ever before.

This book is for you if...

I've worked with over 250 B2B consulting firms, managed service providers, value-added resellers and a bunch of other niche business-to-business specialists in the past 13 years. In taking a diagnostic approach to our working relationship, I've learned the most prevalent challenges they face when looking to install an effective marketing and sales engine in their business.

And I can say with some certainty that the vast majority of companies have a very real problem with positioning, differentiation, and messaging. If you find yourself in that particular boat, this book is definitely for you.

But not everyone is immediately aware that they have this problem. It's not like there's a business inspector constantly looking out for poorly positioned businesses and reaching out to companies with the less-than-welcome feedback that they're duller than Mr. Dull, winner of the dullest dullard in Dullsville.

So, what are some of the tell-tale signs?

You might feel MEH about your business growth, especially when compared with others in your industry. Are you less than happy with the level of brand awareness you're generating? Are you suffering with a low volume of new business leads and enquiries? Do you find it difficult to convert a high number of those opportunities into new business and suffer from multiple objections and price resistance when the conversation turns to the sale?

You might feel MEH about the clients you're working with. Do you find that too many of the inquiries you field (and clients you onboard) are a poor fit or represent a compromise on the ideal client profile you should be aiming for? Perhaps you attract smaller firms than you would wish to work with, with smaller budgets? And perhaps those smaller firms transpire to be the highest maintenance, with every penny scrutinised and every move questioned.

You might feel MEH about your offer and the way that your business is perceived by prospective clients. Perhaps you're aware of the importance of positioning and differentiation and the need to be sufficiently differentiated from competitors. Maybe you've tried to work on your brand, pitch and value proposition but have yet to see the results that a fully optimised market position will bring?

And that's the part I want to dive straight into and address in more detail in this book.

You see, when you fix this type of MEH – the one that deals with positioning, differentiation and messaging, then all the other MEHs fall like dominoes and almost fix themselves.

No more MEH clients.

No more MEH growth.

No more comparisons to MEH competitors.

Positioning and pipeline

I've had the fortune to meet a few positioning sceptics along my journey in marketing; those that doubt any sort of correlation between a company's market position and its ability to attract and convert new customers.

It can be easy to think that this is "fluff" – a distraction from core business development and marketing activities or something already ticked off when the company was launched. Revisiting positioning now seems folly to some. They are fearful that making any sweeping changes would undo all their hard work to date and cause confusion in the minds of would-be clients.

Rest assured that positioning (as I describe in this book) can not only be revisited but dialled up, amplified, polished and even completely overhauled WITHOUT any disruption to current business activities or your ability to keep your currently-MEH pipeline active!

Sorry to be blunt but you're reading this for a reason!

I often use the analogy of the leaky bucket to describe companies (and their marketing efforts) when differentiation is absent and positioning is off-base.

If you pour more water (prospects) into a leaky bucket (a poorly-positioned value proposition), most, if not *all* of them, will drain from the bucket and never be seen again.

In many cases, each lost opportunity represents a substantial amount of revenue lost to competitors and another client that continues to suffer their pains and challenges in the hope that someone else will come save them one day.

How much is each lost opportunity worth to your business?

I've investigated this across a host of clients and prospects. We run the numbers on their "ideal clients", including the recurring revenues and additional fees they can command, not just in up-front or year-one terms but across the lifetime of their engagement.

The average net CLV (customer lifetime value) across the last five clients we did this with?

£144k!

That's the gross profit alone from just ONE client. Imagine losing one or more of those *every month*. That's more than £1.5m in client profits that could be rolling in, simply by fixing the language that greets your prospects wherever your worlds first collide.

By the way, our free ROI Calculator can be found at the web address below along with a downloadable copy of the spreadsheet we use. It could prove to be a real eye opener. There are no forms to opt in or any other hoops to jump through, either.

https://bit.ly/MEHscapologyROI

As we'll establish together, poor positioning causes a raft of "throttling" factors in your sales and marketing pipeline. Each stage of the buyer journey can be adversely impacted in some way or another.

Conversely, what I call "performance positioning" and messaging can increase win rates*, lower price resistance and drive pipelines to new heights.

What's more, it has a compounding beneficial effect through the buyer journey, including the following:

---

* A CSO Insights report found that companies with world-class positioning and messaging close around three times the volume of deals, compared to those without.

- **Improved reach** – more eyeballs on your content, social posts and ads.

- **Higher clickthrough rate** – more visitors to your website, as a result of more compelling calls-to-action.

- **Better conversions** – on landing pages and anywhere that promotes an opt-in or strong connection with the prospect.

- **More opportunities** – if you want more call bookings and appointments with prospects, great positioning helps you do that through an improved understanding of propects' needs and a differentiated offer of help.

- **Higher win rates** – positioning carries through to your sales scripts and pitch decks, resulting in fewer objections and lower price resistance (more prospects become clients).

- **Better client retention** – if you're better positioned to help and attract a specific profile of buyer, they're more likely to stick around for longer or upsell into complimentary solutions, thereby increasing their lifetime value to you.

Attention as a dwindling resource

The proliferation of eager marketers and business development reps have created a hot mess of activity and noise in the online space, making it a pretty noisy and unpleasant place to be sometimes!

Wherever potential buyers congregate, so too do marketers and sales-people. "Fish where the fish are" is the cry of the marketing guru. And so whether you're fishing in "LinkedIn Lake", "Instagram Inlet" or "Email Estuary", the chances are you'll be surrounded by an armada of fellow fisher-folk.

The result is an audience that is increasingly sceptical of any cold (or sometimes even lukewarm) approach.

The bombardment of "same-old, same-old" messaging is causing would-be buyers to feel legitimately targeted and under attack. However valuable and helpful the offer and ultimate product/service offering could be to them, the opportunity may be killed before it's barely had a chance to land.

The challenges aren't restricted to the organic channels, either. The advertising space and particularly the pay-per-click and paid social channels (Facebook Ads, YouTube Ads and LinkedIn Ads) have become more and more expensive as competition has increased. Platforms that once offered successful marketers the opportunity to scale their reach and influence have become a risky game of cat and mouse. A return on investment takes patience, a methodical approach and often some "throwaway" investment to see you through the testing phase. Even when you get it right, the platform will throw curveballs like major algorithm upgrades, privacy changes and changes in its policies for tracking conversions.

Ultimately, whether via organic or paid platforms, your buyers are being force-fed marketing message after marketing message, like unwilling participants in some immersive and perverse version of A Clockwork Orange meets Secret Cinema.

You can be justifiably irked at the position that others have created, with their lazy, over-zealous ways. They're responsible for switching your ideal clients off to anything but a well-crafted and optimised approach and placing you 20 yards behind the start line when attempting to connect with and command the attention of high-value prospects.

We all have to try much, much harder, and be far more inventive if we wish to earn and retain that attention... and it's not getting any easier.

Attention is a scarce resource indeed – and one that we can only hope to earn once we've fully escaped MEH.

The rush to do "more marketing"

The leaders of the consultancies, managed service partners, and other B2B organisations with which I've worked over the past decade and more are often less than enthusiastic about the prospect of working with "another marketing agency".

You see, in way too many cases, they'd had their fingers burnt.

They'd bought into the idea of working with a marketing partner and set expectations very early on about what they could achieve together.

Long story short: *expectations did not match reality*. So, the quest for a consistent, effective marketing strategy continued and the drawing board wheeled out again and given a swift dusting-down.

Does that sound familiar to you?

It amazes me how many established and reputable B2B marketing agencies skip past a new client's proposition and positioning, assuming them to be sound enough. Instead, they often favour campaign strategy, content, and go-to-market tactics that will shine a spotlight on that proposition... whatever state it may be in.

Without that all-important step, the core messaging will fail to land with the right people, compel nobody of sufficient quality and relevance to respond, and could spell disaster for the marketing partnership.

Here's an idea. *Before you entertain the idea of "doing more marketing", take a look at the message you're putting out into the world.* Make sure you're putting your absolute best foot forward, shod in a shiny new pair of gleaming Guccis or Louboutins.

Positioning is the foundational part of your company's marketing arsenal. It's the key that unlocks the potential of ANY channel or tactic you may employ in the future:

- Websites attract more relevant visitors and convert more opportunities.
- Emails get opened and actioned by the right people.
- Ads reach the right people, inspire action and provide an improved return on investment.

Whichever B2B marketing channel or route to market you prefer, I can say with some confidence that its effectiveness can be improved dramatically by feeding it with a fully optimised market position and an un-turn-downable offer before you "switch it on".

You have in your hands the playbook to build that optimised position and un-turn-downable offer. You're ready to do things in the right order, swerve the pain and time sink of the marketing agency merry-go-round, and create the most valuable business asset you'll ever need.

It's not (only) your fault

If you feel that you're solely to blame for your inability to effectively market and grow your business, no book, training course, coaching programme, agency or other solution can help you.

We tell this to prospects, in order for them to believe that there's a solution out there that doesn't have them at the heart of it. That they're not the cog in the machine that needs fixing. You've heard the expression "Nobody likes to be told their baby is ugly"? Well, it turns out that even fewer like to be told that THEY are the ugly one!

In your own positioning and messaging, you'd do well to remember this point, and to get your potential buyers to absolve themselves of whatever blame they harbour, relative to the challenge(s) they face. That way, they'll be more open to getting the help they so sorely need.

By the way, I'll be lifting the lid at various points in this book, going one step further than merely imparting great advice, to tell you why I've included certain arguments and insights. After all, this book is positioning and messaging of sorts, and is fully intended to get you to take action. We'll only achieve that together, if I compel you in the right ways, and you deserve to know the "inner workings" in full.

In the context of your own marketing, here's the less-than-helpful yarn we've been spun...

"More activity" is the answer. Your ultimate aim is brand awareness. Dominate social media, build an email list, fix your lead generation and slap forms on your best stuff, get into Facebook Ads for cheap clicks and "behavioural targeting".

Gary Vaynerchuk and Grant Cardone are two leading influencers on the topics of marketing and sales. I used to respect their opinions more than I do today. At one time, their advice to "hustle" and "be ubiquitous" compelled me to increase my online visibility, flooding the web with my content.

But that was the wrong approach.

You see, they assume that you already have a flawlessly beautiful, blemish-free value proposition. Only after you get your value proposition dialled in, and your positioning and messaging provides a lens through which your ideal clients can see and understand it with ultimate clarity, will "more marketing" serve your needs.

Dan Lok is another influencer who's Marmite to many people (you either love him or can't stand him). He tells a very relevant story about inherited assumptions in his book "F. U. Money"...

A young newlywed was preparing a ham for Christmas dinner. She carefully cut off the end of the ham before placing it in the pan for roasting.

Her husband asked her, "Why did you cut off the end of the ham?" And she replied, "I really don't know. My mother always did, so I thought you were supposed to."

Later, when talking to her mother, she asked her why she cut off the end of the ham before roasting it, and her mother replied, "I really don't know, but that's the way my mom always did it."

A few weeks later while visiting her grandmother, the young woman asked, "Grandma, why is it that you cut off the end of a ham before you roast it?"

Her grandmother replied, "Well, dear, it would never fit into my roasting pan."

You see, all of their lives people do what they're familiar with. They think that, since it's conventional wisdom, "Oh well, that's the way we've been doing it for years" although it's as plain as the nose on their face that it doesn't work. Yet you're supposed to keep doing it that way instead of thinking for yourself.

This book exists because so many companies have failed to think for themselves when it comes to marketing.

They've neglected to give their positioning the focus it deserves and requires to drive success.

Positioning and differentiation are the foundations on which your marketing and sales successes are built.

Get this wrong and it's like building a 12-storey apartment block on inflatable foundations, floating on the Southern Ocean, in a category five storm, with several football sized punctures.

Not exactly solid.

So, the lie that more marketing and brand awareness is the answer to your growth woes should now be in your rear-view mirror. Let's set about fixing the true cause of pipeline pain, once and for all.

The 3 "Pipeline Pains"

1. Same-ism

Same-ism in the business world is when companies start to look and sound like their competitors. This can be a major issue because customers find it difficult to differentiate between them. It can also be a sign that the business is not trying hard enough to stand out from the competition.

There are a few reasons why this might happen. Sometimes, companies may not be able to come up with original ideas, so they simply copy what their rivals are doing. Alternatively, they may not have the resources or time to develop their own unique strategies. In other cases, it might even be due to laziness or a lack of creativity.

Whatever the reason, same-ism can be very damaging for businesses, making it difficult to attract new customers and reducing profits. So, if you're a business owner, it's important to be aware of the dangers of same-ism and make sure you're doing everything you can to stand out from the competition.

The Logo Test

We ask our clients to perform a simple test when assessing whether they're suffering from same-ism: the logo test.

Simply visit the website of a known competitor and do one of two things:

1) Take a screenshot of their homepage and use Photoshop, Canva or a similar design tool to overlay your logo on top of theirs.

or...

2) Just imagine that your logo replaces theirs and that the website is, in fact, your website.

Do the headlines, core messaging and offer still make sense? Could this indeed be an accurate representation of your own website or is it close enough that a complete stranger could mistake their offer for yours?

If so, then you're **not differentiated**. It's one of the starkest reminders that your competitor's proposition is so closely matched to yours that they are taking to YOUR target market. And all other things being equal, they may be winning business from your potential buyers based on price or another factor that shouldn't feature in a smart decision-making process.

Let's investigate this further.

The dangers of mimicking competitors

Here are some tell-tale signs that you may be unwittingly mimicking your competitors:

- Adopting similar branding
- Executing the same marketing strategies
- Using the same product and solution designs
- Enacting the same sales tactics and processes
- Publishing the same headlines, slogans and taglines
- Hiring employees with similar backgrounds and experience levels
- Basing decisions on what the competition is doing
- Taking content inspiration from competitors (blog articles, videos etc.)
- Taking the lead of asupplier/vendor partner and unwittingly mimicking every other channel partner (like the 60,000+ Microsoft Partners across the globe, for example)

Here's the thing: **when companies look and sound the same, buyers often make purchase decisions based on price**. This is because they can't tell the products apart and don't feel like there's much difference between them. They assume that the cheapest option is the best one. You're seen as a commodity and the business goes to the lowest bidder.

Of course, this isn't always the case. Sometimes, the cheapest product is actually the worst one. But it's often difficult for buyers to tell the difference, especially when they're not familiar with the solutions on offer.

If one of your goals is to attract the attention of and work with more "great fit" clients with larger budgets and a more appreciative view of the value your company brings, differentiation will play an even bigger part.

"Different is better than better"

In her book "Fascinate", Sally Hogshead says that "different is better than better". She argues that being different is more important than being better in a business context. This is because most companies are focused on improving their products and services rather than taking steps to stand out from the competition. You should always strive to be *different* from your competitors rather than trying to be *better* than them. It's a lot harder to be different than better, though. That's why the process I outline in this book has been crafted in a structured and logical way: to specifically help you escape *same-ism* and carve a superior path to those competing with you.

However, same-ism isn't the only positioning and differentiation challenge we face today.

2. Tumbleweed Outreach

It's no secret that outreach is one of the most important aspects of any successful "all-bound" (that's inbound + outbound to you) marketing campaign. After all, waiting for customers to come to you can be a drawn-out affair. Some good old outbound messaging, when done well, can help speed things up nicely.

However, many marketers struggle with getting the attention and response they feel they deserve from their prospects. This can be due to a number of factors, such as irrelevant content or messages that are simply so dull that they warrant nothing more than the sound of crickets.

It could also be down to poor targeting; the prospects you're reaching simply aren't a fit for the core value proposition you're pitching to them. There's no excuse for this, as targeting around demographic, firmographic, and behavioural factors has never been easier.

Even when the means to reach your audience is at your fingertips, outreach efforts can be daunting and confusing. Take LinkedIn's ad platform and advanced search targeting, for example. One client we worked with was convinced that they had selected all the relevant criteria to effectively target their ideal buyers by industry, company size, job function/seniority, and more. When we investigated further, however, it transpired that all the Boolean search criteria were worthless. The company was, in fact, targeting ANYONE with a LinkedIn profile! One misplaced "OR" statement had undone all their well-intentioned work.

But there's another reason why your outreach might not be working: namely that you're not *differentiated*. In other words, your message isn't standing out from the rest in the increasingly crowded and noisy marketing landscape.

Whether phone, email, LinkedIn or another type of outreach, a lack of response (I call this "tumbleweed outreach") can cause you to blame the channel and give up on those strategies once and for all.

Consequences of "tumbleweed outreach"

One of the main side effects of poor prospect outreach is that you can quickly become known as a spammer. This can be a major turn-off for potential customers. It can also damage your brand's reputation and the future deliverability of your emails and messages, as more contacts report your messages as spam or block your email domains and profiles from ever darkening their doors again.

Poor outreach is also inherently inefficient, especially when you keep repeating the same approach in the vain hope that success is just around the corner. Why spend time reaching out to prospects who aren't interested in what you have to say? This waste of time and resources can be frustrating. When you outreach to good-fit prospects with irrelevant, boring or undifferentiated content, you're essentially burning bridges with them. By the time you finally crack the best way to perform outreach, your name could be inextricably linked with shady practices in the prospects' minds.

Potential outcomes of tumbleweed outreach include:

- Damage to your brand's reputation
- Turning potential customers off to you and your company
- Wasted time and resources
- Negative impact on the deliverability of future emails and other messages
- Frustration and "imposter syndrome" due to repeated failures

One study by the Content Marketing Institute found that only 27 per-cent of B2B marketers believe that their content is effective. So, it's clear that many companies are struggling with outreach.

It's time to fix this once and for all.

3. MEHssaging

Does your website copy, headline, email signature and other marketing collateral excite you?

If not, then guess what? There's a good chance that your prospects are far from excited, too. Language matters and the messaging you use to represent your business should exude with persuasion!

Lack of novelty, personality and action-oriented language puts potential buyers into their comfort zones. As a result, it will be difficult to "move" them or compel action.

This will be highlighted from several metrics used in your business and will probably be most prevalent in your website analytics.

Bounce rate (the percentage of visitors that leave your site having only hit one page), for example, will be higher on pages and websites where the messaging doesn't tell visitors that they are:

a) In the right place: that the site and its content meet their specific needs and speak to their challenges and situation so that they feel understood.

b) Going to enjoy a unique experience to anywhere else: the novelty factor.

c) In zero doubt as to what to do next: the "journey" has begun. They can see clearly how and why they should take the next step, whether it's submitting an enquiry, downloading content, watching a video or similar.

I'll be talking about language a LOT in this book. Whenever I encourage companies to adopt a new vocabulary (for the purposes of sparking that all-important attention), there are understandable and legitimate concerns about how that may affect discoverability and, specifically, rankings in search engines.

Rest assured, any left-field and "out there" terminology you may adopt in your new positioning is meant only to convert eyeballs into attention and engagement, never to attract the eyeballs in the first place. SEO (search engine optimisation) remains a key marketing strategy for businesses and works completely separately from the task of ditching your MEHssaging.

Think of SEO (or any marketing channel, for that matter) as your party invitation and your language and positioning as the decorations, table dressing and drinks station that greet your partygoers!

No business can afford to allow poor copywriting and dull headlines to torpedo their success. It can destroy trust, create a less-than-stellar impression of your brand and have even the best-fitting prospects fleeing for the door, long before they enjoy the benefits of working with you.

In the pages that follow, we'll get your language dialled up to eleven and primed to generate an embarrassment of attention for your business.

STEP 1:
A Laser-Focused
Target

Great positioning and messaging can only be achieved with context and relevance to the buyer. That means achieving a deep, deep understanding of your ideal buyers.

I've spoken about the "Buyer Brain", which is my dumbed-down way of referring to the very real psychological triggers that, when accounted for in full, leave no valid reason for any good-fit client or customer to say "no" to your offer.

To grab and retain the attention of those buyers, and ensure that we swerve a "Meh" response, we need to VERY quickly invoke two feelings and responses:

1. "This is for me"
2. "You understand me and/or my situation"

The first is the basis of attention. It's what stops the scroll and ensures that your message isn't lost in a sea of noise. It means that you've made it easy for the buyer to see themselves, either in your description of the intended reader/viewer/listener, or the challenges you describe. Your buyers may not recognise your attempts to speak of solutions but they will ALWAYS have a recognition of the challenges they are presently experiencing.

Side note: At any one time, around three percent of your potential buyers will be actively at the consideration or decision stages of the buyer journey, and may recognise the **solutions** you present. Speaking through your messaging about the **challenges and pains** you address will ensure that you engage and are relevant to 100 percent of the recipients.

There's plenty of time later to discuss and prescribe solutions when you're in conversation with your prospective buyers. For now, focus on *understanding the pain*.

The second feeling/response detailed above is an iteration of the first. If you can demonstrate through your language that you have a better-than-most insight into the specific situation faced by the potential buyer, he/she will inevitably feel understood and in good hands.

You've successfully started the journey to becoming known, liked and trusted.

What happens without this understanding?

Without key insights and understanding of the buyer we wish to attract, we will position ourselves either in generics – doing our best to appeal to the crowds of businesses and buyer types that we could help – or we use language that fails to resonate with buyers and instead lumps us right back in with the crowd.

It applies to a great many companies and inevitably leads to this response:

Meh!

The attention we crave which is already so difficult to spark in anyone continues to evade us. Prospects scroll straight past you, cast their eyes elsewhere and find something (or someone) else upon which to focus their gaze.

That's truly devastating for your pipeline, sales and growth plans.

One of the main reasons for this is the assumptions we make with market research. Perhaps it is due to procrastination or avoidance of the hard work necessary but we incorrectly believe that we have a robust understanding of the situation we find our buyers in from our various sales conversations and from the delivery of products and solutions.

That's only true to an extent. We often "colour" our interpretation of the facts with our own experiences and that interpretation transfers to the products and services we offer.

Your questioning during prospect and client conversations, when tailored to your intended sale instead of the broader picture, has the potential to leave large swathes of untapped information in the hearts and minds of the buyer – and a missed opportunity to create a far stronger resonance in future outreach and promotion.

What information are we looking for?

Just what do we need to know about our prospective buyers, so that our subsequent positioning and messaging will hit home hard, jolt them to attention and have them clamouring to speak with us?

Here's a far-from-exhaustive list of ideas:

- Their role and responsibilities in the business
- How they spend their time, both during working hours (the "jobs" they do) and in their personal lives
- Their greatest frustrations in their role
- Aspirations for progression, reward and recognition in their professional life
- Fears about the future, in their role and beyond, relative to the pains and frustrations they encounter
- The tools and products they use in the execution of their job
- The language they use to describe the situation they're in, the challenges they face and the solutions they perceive might help move them forward

The ultimate aim is to have enough insight into the working and waking lives of our buyers that we can easily "step into" their mindset at any time; to create positioning, messaging, assets and content that will appeal on the strongest possible terms to the best-fit buyers we wish to attract. Whether that's through email, social posts, ad creatives, print materials/brochures or another channel. The ability to assume the persona of the potential buyer on command will serve you very well indeed – not just in marketing but in sales and delivery, too, as we achieve and maintain a greater connection with the buyer.

How do we develop "inbound insight"?

In the sections that follow, I'll provide you with the tools and steps required to effectively set up your "Listening Station". Anyone who's spent time digesting the near-endless reams of content coming from HubSpot (the inbound marketing software) will be familiar with the term "inbound hiring". It's not about marketing or sales but instead extols the virtues of having a permanent pipeline of potential candidates for roles in your business.

That not only applies to roles that you're currently advertising for but extends to building your own candidate database that you can dip into at any time, as new roles and requirements arise. This works especially well when you have a rock-solid employer brand and the immediate availability of candidates becomes less important than finding the right bum for the right seat.

I'm going to suggest something similar... **inbound insight!**

I'm a huge fan of the concept of "always be polling". Surveys and assessments, gathering data points, facts and figures, as well as more personal insights about our target audience should be a consistent and ongoing commitment; not just when we're trying to position our business or create our value proposition.

This means running email and social media outreach campaigns that connect with your ideal prospects without giving off that overtly salesy stench that accompanies so many on LinkedIn and email. This will gather valuable intel from prospects and can continue to run in the background of your day-to-day business operations.

When you need those insights, you can just dip in and drink from the firehose.

OK, so let's get more specific about what we're covering in this first step.

Three things:

1. Segmentation
2. The buyer persona (reframed)
3. Proven pain

I'm going to bring some new thinking to the idea of positioning by making any position malleable to the specific buyer profile that stands before you in any given marketing or sales situation. You'll learn that MEHscapology is not necessarily about positioning the entire company (and certainly not about restricting your efforts to just one niche) but about acquiring flexibility in the moment to ensure your messaging lands squarely and solidly every time.

You'll learn how to gather challenges like a pro and how the information you receive is vital to the success of any marketing or sales effort – especially in your efforts to escape MEH and speak with power and authority to any potential buyer via any channel.

So, with an open mind and a willingness to truly connect with more buyers more regularly, let's proceed!

A Different Segment

At times when writing this book, I'm aware of the need to discuss some very MEH subjects. This is one of them. It's MEH because you've heard it all before.

I'm talking about *niching*.

We've all been told, countless times and from countless sources, that specificity in your market and in your marketing will yield greater results.

And it will. It comes back to resonance – having your message felt, received, understood, and seen as ultimately relevant to the perfect recipient. This specificity drives response and action-taking – the sorts of things we seek and hope for in any prospective buyer.

And yet... like a scene from *The NeverEnding Story*, through these pages I hear your cries...

"I don't want to *niche*!"

It's at what level you choose to *niche* that will impact how damaging or rewarding the level of specificity in your business will prove to be.

As we emerged from the COVID pandemic that swept the globe from 2020 onwards, one of the many lessons that period taught us is that niching can be a risky business.

Any business that niched solely to serve companies in the travel and hospitality industries rapidly discovered that. Those sectors saw huge and incredibly damaging challenges land on their doorstep, with customers and revenue disappearing literally overnight.

Suppliers to companies in these sectors saw their contracts paused or cancelled, as many struggled to keep the lights on. And it wasn't the right time to be holding people to their contractual obligations or threatening legal proceedings.

Segment resonance

There are many surprises in business and a lack of diversification in your client portfolio can leave you unnecessarily exposed.

So, we don't *niche*. We segment.

It's the best of both worlds. We get to present a highly-targeted, relevant and compelling message to a specific buyer type without communicating to the world that this is the only industry vertical or business profile that we work with.

This isn't about positioning the whole business for any one niche but instead about putting the best argument together for a specific profile of buyer, so that when they find you, they connect, pay attention and are compelled to respond. This is what I call "segment resonance".

Segment resonance ensures that we earn the highest levels of attention and intrigue from our target buyers. We compel them to respond and engage with our content and calls to action and, ultimately, identify themselves as an ideal fit for our products and solutions.

I want to stress at this point that we're still talking about the traits attributable to a target company or an "account". Segmentation and your approach to it should filter down from company level – where we unearth the desired characteristics of a perfect client organisation – to the "buyer persona" level, represented by the individuals therein.

So how do we achieve it?

If you've been around the marketing landscape for any amount of time, you'll be familiar with landing pages. These typically sit deeper in your website than your homepage or other "top level" pages and usually serve to present a specific offer to a specific profile of visitor.

On your homepage, you need to be all things to all people. If you are able to work with a broad range of business types and in multiple sectors, you must present a broad, somewhat generic presence at that level of your site.

On a landing page, however, it's essential that you present a specific, highly focused opportunity to a relevant visitor. This could be a webinar replay opt-in page, for instance, where the presentation focuses on "how healthcare companies can improve efficiency and halve their costs by fixing three core elements in their organisation".

It's obvious who this offer is targeted at and the challenge it is intended to solve. The challenge thereafter is to drive these buyer types to this page, so we can begin the journey of engaging them, first online, then offline – but how to drive that traffic is a topic for another book!

A simple 3-step checklist for segment fit

There are countless variables to consider when selecting the criteria for the ideal client organisation. I would encourage any business leader to build a "prospect fit matrix" that outlines the various identifying factors: not only the firmographic elements, such as company size, location, etc. but also some of the attitudinal aspects – perhaps the beliefs and language you encounter in dealing with a great-fit company, for instance.

In lieu of a more detailed and extensive matrix, however, you can start by assessing how well they meet the following three simple characteristics. This will ensure that you're dealing with a prospective client that shows characteristics that are becoming of a profitable "stayer" in your client stable:

1. **They're "targetable"**

   This is imperative but is overlooked so often by marketers. Long before you jump to "promotion mode" and start running campaigns for your target audience (and even before you set your market position in stone), you'd do well to confirm your ability to reach their eyeballs via whatever channel or channels you consider most likely to bear fruit.

This way, you will find it easy to slide your offer under their noses either by organic or paid means. You'll need to consider the various digital and offline interfaces between you and the buying segment. It's very much a case of "fish where the fish are" and you may need to do some digging so that you can feel confident in your chosen route to market later on.

Let's say, for example, as is often the case in B2B, that your audience hangs out on LinkedIn. If you have access to their advanced search functions, which usually come with a paid Sales Navigator subscription, you can provide all the identifying factors as search criteria. You'll easily see just how many ideal-fit accounts there are in your target sector or market segment – in essence, your "target addressable market" but at a greater level of detail and relevance.

2. They're in the ascendancy

Another essential characteristic for your target segment is a growing market sector. There are exceptions to this rule (you may provide services that aid ailing companies or those facing times of commercial hardship) but, for the most-part, you'll want to ensure that prospective clients face few external growth constraints or environmental/political pressures that would put a long-term, smooth and profitable partnership in jeopardy.

A growing market also suggests that this target client is more likely to have money to invest – another essential factor that isn't always obvious from the outside. And so we look for clues that allude to their ability and willingness to invest.

They may, for example, be advertising jobs in key growth roles, such as sales and customer success/account management. They may have recently moved into a larger office in a prime location. They may be posting some of their recent client wins and new business wins (not always a public announcement scenario). Simply put, where there are clues to their investment in growth, there's more likelihood that this prospect will see the value in what you have to offer.

3. **They're "challenge fatigued"**

I go far deeper into the challenge/problem side of things in a later section. For now, let's just say that you MUST position yourself to speak to a legitimate and painful challenge that your ideal buyers face. Not only are they experiencing a problem that you can help to solve but they are so affected by it that they are compelled to do something about it.

They're not simply in "research mode" but have suffered long enough for anything but a workable and proven solution to be completely off the cards.

At a company level, there will be recurring themes – challenges that plague a particular sector or segment of the prospect pool. These could be regulatory, political or commercial. Many companies are plagued by a particular timescale or zeitgeist moment – for example, the introduction of new compliance rules that present an industry-wide problem to every company operating therein.

To ensure your target client is "challenge fatigued", use some of the outreach and "always be polling" strategies I speak about later in the book to gain the most thorough understanding possible.

The importance of tone

In working with a good number of B2B consultancies and managed service providers in recent years, I've encountered some resistance to the more outlandish and different language I prescribe. Some of them feel that the language won't land with an audience that is more staid or conservative while others believe a more left field approach will work.

Why the disparity?

Different buyers and company profiles will expect differing tones and personalities in their partners and suppliers. Getting this wrong could adversely impact your perceived credibility and status in the buyer's eye.

Consider the tone and likely cultural aspects of a company sector that may influence their communication preferences. This could impact the ways in which you target them but also in the style and manner in which you approach them.

Cultural aspects of a business operation can also influence where they hang out and where they conduct business. In the real world, for example, you're unlikely to go seeking out your next romantic date at a funeral (though fans of Will Ferrell in the movie Wedding Crashers may think otherwise). The same goes for marketing and prospecting. Partners at an accountancy firm are unlikely to be showcasing the latest dance craze on Tik Tok, much less using it to seek out their next professional services partner.

An ABM-inspired way to pick your target segment(s)

The term ABM, has been peddled by many well-known marketing brands in recent years as the next big thing. In reality, it's been around for many years and is simply enjoying a renaissance. Like in the world of fashion, all things marketing do go in cycles, after all!

ABM stands for Account-Based Marketing. This is a highly-focused methodology for identifying, connecting with and engaging target accounts that you wish to do business with. It's a proactive or aggressive approach to marketing that hones in on a specific segment of great-fit companies (accounts) that demonstrate the very criteria that determines suitability for your offering.

ABM has many benefits but chief among them is the ability to connect with and influence not just one but *many* key decision makers in committee-based purchasing environments. The idea is to achieve high "account penetration" by forging a relationship with multiple contacts in the target organisation, all or many of whom would have a say in whether or not to engage a company like yours, for the kinds of projects and solutions on offer.

In the context of MEHscapology and achieving an unparalleled understanding of your target buyers, we're only interested (for now) in the process of selecting your target accounts, which might look something like this...

Step #1: Build an extensive list of target accounts

Leave no stone unturned in your quest for target companies. Many of them you'll already know. In addition to the methods and sources listed below, you can go ahead and jot down the companies that you have long-since decided you absolutely HAVE to work with. You know the ones. You've been courting them, at least in dreams, for what seems like a lifetime.

Once you've listed the dream team, use the following sources to supplement your list, adding as many suspects as you can:

- **Your existing contact database or CRM system**
  If you've been doing any sort of marketing or lead generation before now, including any offline activities, networking and events, you'll already have a bunch of companies that you have some sort of connection with.
  These may need to be prioritised as an awareness and recognition of your brand will be hugely beneficial when it comes to outreach and the presentation of your offer later on. It's the natural place to start.

- **Tracked visitor information** (from tools such as HubSpot's prospecting module or Leadfeeder)
  Many tools out there help to identify companies visiting your website, which, let's face it, is a good indication that you're "on their radar". Many are available on trial, so you can start to assemble a list of visiting accounts. Again, it means that you won't be trying to develop the relationship from a completely cold start.

- **Intent and trigger data**
  Companies like LeadSift and Bombora provide what's known in marketing and sales circles as "intent data". These are insights sourced from a variety of platforms and locations that, when

combined, provide signals as to the likelihood of a user or company having a particular challenge or actively being in the market for a product or solution.

As mentioned earlier, at any one point in time, around 3 percent of your target market occupy the "active buyer" stage of the journey. They're considering their options in a big way and are likely to pull the trigger on a solution purchase within the next 30-90 days... according to those in intent data circles.

Once you've exhausted all of your "owned" or otherwise influenced contacts, this would be a solid option for supplementing your target list.

- **LinkedIn Sales Navigator search or company data and contact sources, such as Zoominfo and Experian**

  You can also acquire valuable data using a search that tells the source (LinkedIn or another third-party provider) which firmographic data is important to you and which denotes a likely fit, based on industry, location, size, etc.

  Again, this is a great way to supplement your target list once you've exhausted those prior sources.

Consider segmentation or tagging, as well as the qualification stages that apply to your "owned" (opted in) companies. Also, factor in any lead scoring system that you may have in place – i.e. the process by which you prioritise leads, based on their interactions with your site and other marketing assets to date.

Step #2: Tier your prospects

Segment your target accounts further by considering the criteria most important to you – whether that's logos and "fame" clients, local companies that offer some face-to-face benefit or the strength of prior connection and their existing awareness of your brand.

A <u>suggested</u> segmentation might look something like this:

Tier A targets (×100)

- Have a history of communication with your company, or...
- Demonstrate high levels of buyer intent through their behaviours, or...
- Would just look fantastic on your "Happy clients" web page – a recognised and respected logo that will make any competitor green with envy

Tier B targets (×1,000)

- No prior interaction with you but has visited your website (trigger), or...
- Has shown recent behaviour that indicates suitability or readiness for your offering (e.g. a hire into a key growth role, an office move or a recent successful funding round) or...
- Simply fits the firmographic profile of an ideal client – a good size, HQ location and a demonstrable history of engaging expert assistance from outside, such as yours

Tier C targets (everyone else)

- Has a pulse. Seriously, though, this segment would comprise any companies that largely fit the firmographic profile of a good (if not ideal) client or is likely to meet the criteria in the near future.

There's an important caveat I would throw in at this point. Whilst it's a good idea to populate all three tiers, so that you always have some activity in your pipeline and don't restrict influence, all the business you will ever need can easily come from tiers A and B.

If you're in an advisory business, for instance, it's likely that you're focused on relationship-based selling, taking the position as trusted advisor rather than salesperson and placing a heavy focus on client delight – increasing the already-high lifetime value further through retention.

Build your list and start off by scanning the names in Tier A. Get intimately familiar with them and sear their names and logos into your brain. Get excited at the prospect of working with them, visualising the perfect engagement. You're on the way to fully understanding your target audience and their needs.

PARTNER STORY – The Wow Company

With a name like The Wow Company, you might expect to hear about a firm that helps businesses to market themselves better – or perhaps an extreme sports travel agent?

But you'd be wrong. They're a firm of *accountants*!

I've been a happy client of theirs for more than seven years and they've certainly produced many Wow moments in that time. In fact, I'm doing a massive disservice by referring to them as just "accountants", as they offer a whole range of business advisory services for a very specific profile of client.

As they attest to on their own website, they LOVE agencies.

Very early on, the leadership team at Wow recognised the importance and value of niching and set out to identify a business category that was:

- Under-served in the accountancy space
- Enjoyable to work with
- Able to match their own "vibe" and allow them to be authentic.

Marketing agencies ticked all the boxes, so Wow commenced a journey to really understand this group of clients, adding services to solve the specific challenges they faced. Years later, they are recognised here in the UK as THE go-to accountancy firm for marketing agencies with 8-80 staff. They offer a specialist service to a specialist audience and their years of focus mean that they can truly claim to be the best in the world at what they do.

What's interesting now is watching Wow emulate their success with agencies in another niche: consultancies. Whilst there are similarities between agencies and consultancies, there are differences too and they matter. It's been impressive watching how Wow has worked hard to build the additional expertise required in this new niche. Their positioning is once again backed up by their delivery, which helps them cement their dominant position in the market.

A Different Buyer

If you've researched best marketing practices or undergone market-ing training before now, there's a very good chance that you've been told to focus on a specific and relevant "buyer persona".

The concept is sound and I'm not about to debunk this approach but, before we go any further, I'd like to address this rather damaging lan-guage. The words "persona" or "avatar" (a popular alternative term) seem to dehumanise the individual.

At a time when we really should be creating an unbreakable bond and deep understanding of our buyers, we're already giving them a rather faceless description. You could argue that the term "buyer" lands them with an identity that centres solely around their monetary value to you, too.

So, before we go any further, here's my tip. Where you see words like persona, avatar or buyer, replace them with the word "person". There's an inherent respect that comes with seeing someone as a human being, even within a commercial setting.

People do business with people and this small gesture sets the tone for a meeting of equals, which in the world of B2B marketing and sales, is imperative. It could just be the difference between welcom-ing a new client and waving them away into the arms of your fiercest competitor.

Why is a "person focus" important?

The most important feeling to invoke in any would-be client is that "this is for me" or "they really understand me" when they receive your proposition. Whether it's in the form of an ad, email or face-to-face pitch, this initial response is the very basis of attention.

If you cannot invoke this feeling, your prospect has already scrolled past you, literally or metaphorically speaking.

To gain such a deep understanding and be able to call it to mind in any situation, is to consistently (and on command) create the messaging and supporting content that resonates with your customers wherever and whenever your brand is in front of them.

Knowing their most pressing challenges, ambitions and language that your prospect is experiencing aids the creation of content and messaging that not only resonates but compels customers to respond.

Person selection

It's important to be specific about the people that your solutions can best help and for whom you'll be able to generate the very best results. However, it's just as important for those that you cannot help to see that your solutions are not for them.

This act of filtering will help to keep your pipeline free from poor-fit "tyre kickers" who could take up your precious time even though you're just not right for each other.

In the world of recruitment, this looks like "hire slow, fire fast" but in reverse. We want people to disqualify themselves early to minimise the impact on your pipeline... and your diary!

Most businesses have three to five core profiles they wish to deal with: distinct types of individuals that represent those that you want many more of in your sales pipeline.

When considering which person profiles you wish to focus on, by all means consider those who represent the best "end clients". But also consider referrers, partners and influencers: those who can connect you with more end buyers at scale.

These could include the heads of industry associations, admins of LinkedIn Groups (the members of which meet the criteria of your ultimate client) or "highly visible" subject matter experts. In each case, potential partners must have no competing solution on offer that could conflict with yours.

Here's what a group of person profiles might look like for ABC Consulting:

1. Chief Technology Officers at financial services companies in the UK with 500 to 5,000 employees

2. Chief Financial Officers at financial services companies in the UK with 500 to 5,000 employees

3. Executive Assistants to the CEOs at those same financial services companies

4. Admins of LinkedIn Groups, the members of which are senior leaders in mid-sized financial services companies

You may think that persons 1 and 2 can be bundled up. Couldn't we just target CXOs at those companies?

No. And here's why...

CTOs and CFOs have VERY different concerns, responsibilities, and face very different challenges in their roles.

CTOs are concerned with building a technology capability that supports the productivity and efficiency of the business. They are interested in having the best technology integrated across the company, with maximum uptime, empowering staff to do their best work.

Meanwhile, the CFO is concerned with profitability and the overall financial health of the business. They may choose to buy into the CTO's strategy and support their ambitions financially but they may also insist on an extensive RFP process to get the best deal. They may go so far as to curb spend in certain areas to protect the bottom line.

So, they have very different responsibilities, priorities, and points of view. They, therefore, require very different messages and language, to appeal to disparate goals and ambitions.

This specificity of understanding and messaging will yield far better results and conversion rates later, as you'll spark that "this is for me" moment in each individual, earn their attention and likely follow up with a better-targeted call-to-action.

Why include the Executive Assistant? Shouldn't we go exclusively for decision makers?

Those in CXO roles are big targets for marketers and prospectors the world over. By the time you reach the end of this book, your offer will be so appealing to these senior leaders that higher levels of attention will be inevitable. But many are so awash and overwhelmed with the constant barrage of incoming emails and inMails (paid-for LinkedIn direct messages) that they often pass the responsibility to juniors.

The responsibility for researching new suppliers could fall on the Executive Assistant or someone at a lower management level. He or she will do the legwork in advance of the "chief" getting involved.

For that reason, one or more of your ideal person profiles may be a maven or influencer at a more junior level. Don't forget them. Don't undervalue them. Many B2B purchase decisions are made by committee and this junior person may be your best friend in your quest to conquer the boardroom.

Aside from the demographic factors, how else might we consider and decide on our best prospects to connect with?

One method I would recommend employing is to look at your existing and past client base. Identify those that you loved working with the most and would happily clone if the technology becomes available. In short, *which clients do you want more of?*

Here are some suggested factors for consideration when selecting the best "target" person profiles:

- **Revenue and profit** – which clients have allowed you to charge what you're worth (or more) and be most profitable? What combination of individual and company profile gives you the most confidence that you will "get paid"?

- **Enjoyability factor** – which client types do you enjoy working with because they're in an exciting niche, culturally sound, value your expertise to a greater degree, etc?

- **Referral potential** – which internal or external "customers" can put you in front of more potential buyers by referral or recommendation? This could be another department or business unit in a large organisation or a fellow member of a relevant organisation. Whatever it is, the potential may extend far beyond just your working relationship.

- **Star factor** – do any clients offer great PR potential? A case study or testimonial from THAT company may catapult you into the consciousness of a similarly high-profile logo in future and might represent a huge step up in the size of organisation (and size of deal) that you work on.

Demographic, firmographic and psychographic factors

I want to get through this segment rather quickly. In a book that promises to help you escape MEH, this part sails dangerously close to being incredibly MEH all by itself.

There are, though, a great many marketers out there providing questionable advice on how to best identify and target buyers. They tell you to build a target profile that includes elements like the last film the person saw, the car they drive, their favourite book, etc.

It doesn't take a genius to work out just how ridiculous this is.

A quick exercise: bring to mind someone you know who occupies a similar role to yours. If you're a consultancy owner, the chances are good that you know another consultancy owner in a business of a similar profile and size.

Now, consider the likelihood that they drive the same car as you, that the last movie they saw at the cinema is the same as yours, that they read the same book, that they drink the same beer, that they wear the same brand of clothes.

You get the idea. None of this matters.

Modern marketing channels allow for some pretty fantastic targeting If you were using Facebook ads to reach your next buyer, you'd be able to use their love of certain brands, celebrities and media, to laser focus your approach.

But how useful is that in B2B marketing?

Rant over. Let's look at some factors that might be more useful in helping you determine the best channels and promotional strategies:

Demographic factors – your best buyers may conform to a set of demographic elements that will help you to better focus your understanding of your market and match your message to their needs. Elements like age, gender, location, first language all aid you in tailoring your tactical approach to reaching your audience.

Firmographic factors – this is the set of characteristics used to segment companies and organisations into defined groups, which we covered in the last section. In short, this is the account-level data which, when used in conjunction with the individual's demographic data, will ensure that you're reaching the right person at the right profile of company.

You can use this data to evaluate the total addressable market (TAM) before you even kick off a marketing effort, and to assess target account suitability – great when you know the specific companies you wish to do business with, as in an account-based marketing (ABM) strategy.

Psychographic factors – this is a deeper level of profiling. You may never use it but it can be useful when dialling in your messaging to appeal at an emotional level with prospects.

Elements of psychographic data include personality traits, lifestyle choices, interests and hobbies, beliefs and values. It's folly to think that these factors will be shared by large swathes of people in a specific role. Not all CTO's will be Star Wars Cosplayers who enter "Jedi" into the religion field on their local census form! But there may be some loose trends and recurring themes that can help you develop a closer connection.

How to build your ideal target profile

I use a bunch of frameworks that I've developed to pull together the required information to achieve a fully differentiated position and un-turn-downable offer.

The first deals with buyer profiles and is split into three sections:

1. **Buyer demographics** – this largely mimics LinkedIn's advanced search criteria. If you've ever used the Sales Navigator product, you'll be familiar with this.

2. **Trigger and goals** – this framework helps you to delve into the buyer's mind and establish their primary drivers – the reasons why they might need your solutions and, more importantly, the "triggers" that will ultimately decide whether they simply research you or buy from you.

3. **The buyer's voice** – what's the language that your ideal prospects use, in relation to the challenges and pains that they experience? How would you or any referring partner recognise a prospect by what they say and how they say it?

Let's look at the first of these in more detail before we address the others in the next section.

Buyer demographics

Consultancies, professional services firms, managed services companies and the like all tend to have a very good sense of what an ideal buyer looks like to them. Many that I speak to are seeking to get the attention of larger companies, in the hope that those with more complex requirements and who are "playing a bigger game" will have the budgets to match.

To identify larger prospects is to focus on demographic and firmographic factors like the number of employees or, where available, turnover/revenue.

At an individual level, many also know the best roles to connect with, for a meaningful conversation about a working alliance. That could be the ultimate decision-maker or someone more junior with influence over the selection and engagement of new suppliers and partners.

It tends to comprise a range of job titles or a combination of job functions and seniority levels.

Many marketers over-complicate this step of the process. Instead of sticking to the simple demographic factors, they dive deep into contrived and often ill-researched psychographic factors. Whilst that might serve the B2C marketer, who has to account for huge numbers of potential buyers – the "stack 'em high, sell 'em low" approach – that's not going to cut it in B2B. It's simply surplus to requirements.

Let's remind ourselves why we're doing this and where it later serves us.

Targeting.

One of the key factors in market selection, often overlooked by those in the marketing space, is the "reachability" of those ideal buyers. If you can't slide your proposition right under their noses, then you're going to find it very difficult to engage them in sufficient numbers to make an impact on your pipeline and sales.

Provided your lead message connects with the prospect and elicits the desired response, you'll be enjoying many conversations that lead to opportunities and sales more consistently.

How do you know you've selected the right profile of target prospect?

It goes without saying that anyone you wish to engage through your marketing and outreach efforts should be a great fit for the solutions that you offer. A diagnostic approach later will determine their needs so, for the time being, we simply need to focus on the companies and individuals with the size, budget, level of responsibility and other characteristics necessary to qualify.

The issue of *need* can also be addressed in your positioning and messaging. If you speak about project management issues, for example, and specifically the topic of "project recovery", then your message is likely to appeal to, and generate a response from, those that feel that their project is in need of recovery.

Need coupled with our demographic and firmographic segmentation can help ensure that we have conversations with those we can help the most.

In short, relentlessly aim to create the "this is definitely for me" response in your prospects. That is the basis of attention, which is a scarce currency and becoming scarcer by the minute. Elicit that feeling and you're ahead of many who might be competing for the attention of the same individual(s).

Action:

Create the prospect profile that you feel best suits your ideal target. Specificity wins in this game and will help you generate the requisite level of resonance. Remember; once you've mastered a position and un-turn-downable offer for this prospect profile, you can replicate the same strategy for others you can serve.

CLIENT STORY – Smarter Not Harder

I knew from their company name that these guys would be an open and willing participant in the process of MEHscapology. This was further evidenced by their no-nonsense approach to productivity optimisation for their clients.

But their proposition was let down ever so slightly by the sub-optimal way in which it was presented to prospects via their website and other marketing channels. The leadership team were also bringing a new proposition to market – designed to maximise the referral potential of their clients – that they wanted to generate the greatest buzz and impact around.

Now, herein lay the challenge. Whilst Smarter Not Harder (SNH) had bags of success and experience with enterprise level clients with all the social proof, case studies and testimonials that accompany that success, the new service was intended for an SMB (small to medium business) market.

In the earlier discovery phase, we identified the mis-match between social proof and target buyer. We knew they would have to change their approach to meet the needs of a new profile of client. The "household name" client logos would scare most, if not all, SMB prospects away as they would assume that the solution (and, more importantly, the fees involved) would be wildly inappropriate for a company like theirs.

We started by recognising that the needs and messaging appeal of their new audience were a far cry from the persona they embodied. No more showcasing and talking about the behemoth clients they'd worked with. By reaching out and listening to the SMB market, they could identify the main language and positioning needs to a far greater depth.

During this phase, SNH were even able to determine the optimal number of salespeople in the target organisation to achieve the greatest resonance and interest levels in their offering: laser-focused targeting!

As a result, SNH was able to build a solid pipeline of SMB opportunities that will see them dominate the "sales opportunity activation" space for years to come.

A Different Challenge

You'll find people in marketing talk a lot about the "buyer's pain".

To my mind, every company in the world is in the business of transformation. Whatever products or solutions you're selling, you're typically taking your buyer from a situation they're currently experiencing WITHOUT your solution toward a more attractive and compelling future state that only exists WITH your solution. You provide the mechanism, tools or pathway to do that.

The implication is that they're currently experiencing a less-than-optimal existence. There is some sort of shortcoming or lack, a challenge or pain that they're currently living with that they would rather eradicate forever.

The best marketers and salespeople take a diagnostic approach to understanding the challenges that their prospects are encountering, in order to prescribe the very best solution.

The less successful ones go out assuming that any prospect they're in conversation with needs their product and solution and is somewhat baffled when they get rebuffed.

Imagine going to your doctor, and they say "OK, here are your pills", before asking you to describe any of your symptoms. They would be struck off for gross negligence and so should anyone in business that attempts a similar approach!

Collect challenges

Here's my challenge to you. Understand your buyers and the challenges they face, relative to your area of expertise, at a deeper level and to a better extent than they understand themselves.

How do we do that?

Always be polling.

Now, I'm going to go out on a limb and assume that you've been in business a while. If you've read this far, there's a good chance that you're trying to fix a challenge in your business relating to attracting buyer attention.

This isn't your first rodeo and you've networked, schmoozed and sold your way into a number of working relationships and partnerships before.

But every touchpoint with a prospect, client or partner is an opportunity to learn.

If you had to guess, how many touch points (emails, social messages, phone calls) have you had in the past year?

Even if it were just one a week, that's more than 50 opportunities to ask the question, "What's your biggest challenge right now?".

With 50 responses, you already have sufficient data to identify what the recurring themes and trends are with what's troubling your target market.

We regularly go out to connections on LinkedIn, to our email list, and in the daily calls we have with prospects, clients and partners. We like to keep the responses as "real" as possible and focus primarily on the individuals that best represent our ideal clients – those we want more of in our client stable.

Sometimes, we have a sufficiently warm connection to guarantee a response. On other occasions, where the connection is in its infancy or somewhat colder, we'll offer to buy them one of those expensive frothy coffees as an incentive. Even at £3 or £4 a time, the value of the insight far outweighs the price of the drink.

Got a bunch of responses?

Next, we need to extract the value from the data. At present, we just have a bunch of (often garbled) responses, in various formats, of differing lengths and levels of detail. We need to *identify the themes*.

This part is tricky. The themes will depend entirely on the context of your business and the profile of buyers that you reach out to.

Let me give you an example.

In a recent effort to reach out and learn from our own prospects, we gathered 100+ responses from senior marketers, salespeople and executives in B2B consulting and managed service firms in the UK and US (our primary markets).

We asked them for their greatest challenge relating to marketing and sourcing new business.

Responses varied, with a number of challenges related to marketing technology, resourcing, strategy and more. But two themes emerged more often than any others...

Attribution and Attention

Many respondents faced challenges with reporting on the most important marketing metrics and determining where their best leads and clients were coming from. That's *attribution*.

However, the most prevalent challenge in our target market was earning and retaining the *attention* of great-fit prospects of the quality and volume required to achieve their growth goals.

Armed with this knowledge, we knew that if we created a solution to help those buyers to master their positioning and messaging, to put a more compelling proposition in front of more great-fit buyers and generate a greater response into the bargain, we'd be onto a winner.

Spoiler alert: We weren't wrong!

Other sources of intel

If you prefer a slightly more introverted approach to intelligence gathering, there are plenty of other sources of valuable information that you can access from the comfort of your ergonomic office chair.

If there's any demand at all for the products and services you offer, there's a very good chance that many researchers and buyers are jumping onto Google (or other search engines) and searching for information on a variety of related topics.

The great news for you in your search for prospect pains and challenges is that those search phrases and keywords are analysed. The demand for each is shown to users of Google's advertising platform – and you can obtain this intel without spending a penny.

Google's Keyword Planner features allow you to research demand for topics related to your offering and see how many users are out there searching for your expertise. As well as generic keywords, there will inevitably be searches that provide clues about the underlying challenges these users are facing.

For example:
A search for the term "brand positioning" shows several related keywords that include words like "strategy" and "process", indicating that many people are unsure of how to go about achieving a strong position in their market.

Good job I wrote this book then, eh?!

This tool, as well as Google Trends (trends.google.com) can show you just how the demand changes over time – whether you're focusing on a need that is diminishing or growing in popularity. This can be crucial for optimising the timing of your positioning exercise and subsequent relaunch.

Prospect pains often reveal themselves, too, in the questions people ask online. To that end, two more sites to be aware of are answerthepublic.com and quora.com. Not only can these sites inform your positioning around highly relevant challenges faced by users but also direct your later content strategy, when search engine rankings and brand discoverability become your primary aim.

There are also many specialist online forums and social media groups (on LinkedIn, for example) that will be jam-packed full of clues: questions, complaints and rants and content shared amongst members all provide valuable intel on what's important to that collective. As always, relevance is key, so the title and positioning of the group or forum, as well as a cursory glance of member profiles for due diligence, would be a good idea. You can quickly assess the suitability of groups and the likely quality of insights gained before trawling through their musings.

Assumed vs. Acquired intel

After you've exhausted the sources that focus heavily on the "straight from the horse's mouth" approach, you can then turn to your own observations on the market.

Many readers will have operated in business for some considerable time and you'll have rubbed shoulders with prospects and clients alike on many occasions. You'll have been that willing ear when they tell you their problems – not always with the specific intention of capturing and logging those problems for your own purposes. But those insights will have registered on some conscious or subconscious level. You are, therefore, a reliable and valuable source of intel yourself.

So, what problems have you helped clients overcome to date?

What are the recurring or emerging trends among those challenges? If the majority of your clients could fix one big problem in their business, what would it be?

We'll use these insights to feed into the frameworks that follow.

We'll also create a new "language library" later that you'll use to refer to these challenges in a new and different way, to appeal to your buyers in a more compelling way than any competitor does.

For now, your homework is to capture as many legitimate prospect and client challenges as possible. Here's a matrix you can use to do just that...

The Prospect Pains Matrix

There are four quadrants to populate with the intel you've gathered, according to your prospect's situation: the "now" position to the left, moving to the "future" desired state on the right.

1. Triggers

In this space, we capture the challenges and reasons for a prospect wanting to take action. It's "the straw that breaks the camel's back" – the pain and undesirable outcomes, so strong that they can't possibly live with them anymore. The frustration has built to such a level that they absolutely must act.

This feeling is present in every legitimate buyer of any solution or service, though the levels of pain may vary.

Oftentimes, we may need to probe further into an expressed challenge or pain to uncover the true "trigger". A game of "Five Whys" can help us get to the true root cause or strongest pain.

Sakichi Toyoda, the Japanese industrialist, inventor and founder of Toyota Industries, developed the Five Whys technique in the 1930s. It became popular in the 1970s and Toyota still uses it to research and solve problems today.

It's a simple process to delve deeper into an expressed challenge by asking "why?". An example might help...

A prospective client complains that "Our CRM system is ineffective".

On the face of it, this may seem like a legitimate problem to note as a "trigger". So, we proceed on the assumption that we've unearthed some valuable insight.

But what if that statement is only symptomatic of the true issue at hand? Let's ask *why* the prospect's CRM system is ineffective.

Response: "It's not giving us accurate forecasting. The sales we forecast never bear any relation to the results we attain".

OK, better, but perhaps we need to delve deeper. "Why is forecasting so inaccurate?".

Response: "Not every interaction is getting logged and leads are often shown as being at the wrong stage of qualification. This means they miss out on key communications and follow-ups".

"Why aren't interactions getting logged?".

Response: "Our sales staff tend to default to other methods to track and manage their leads. Sometimes it's spreadsheets and sometimes a third-party system that they've acquired of their own volition".

"Why are they defaulting to their own methods rather than the prescribed CRM system?".

Response: "We didn't really involve the sales team in the CRM selection process and the training was pretty light. As a result, adoption of the technology has been poor".

OK, so after Five Whys, we've uncovered the true cause of pain. It's not simply that the CRM system is ineffective but that staff weren't included in the selection and implementation of the CRM system. Adoption is the challenge not the technology.

It's hugely important to get to the root cause as your diagnosis not only determines your market position and messaging to connect with your desired audience but also helps prescribe the most effective solution and deliver legitimate value to every client you choose to serve.

The Five Whys won't only help you identify the true pains of your target buyers but also their true fears, goals and ambitions.

2. Fears

Now, I'm going to need to ask you to promise something.

When you learn this next part of the process and I lift the lid on why and how marketers use this information, you have to assure me that you'll only use your newly acquired powers for good and not evil!

You see, a great many marketers prey on the fears and insecurities of their would-be buyers to "scare them" into buying.

But that doesn't work if you want to run (and keep running) a successful consultancy or similar B2B company. Karma has a reputation for catching up with you and that was well before the age of Trustpilot, Google Reviews and Glassdoor!

I'm going to show you how to establish the deepest fears of your buyers to use that insight for good.

How do we do that?

I've been pretty open about the need to use a diagnostic approach in positioning, marketing and sales. Whilst you could go down the route of many in marketing and "agitate" the pain that your prospect encounters, there's a far more effective, gratifying and downright less sleazy way of using the intel.

And that's to ensure that you propose and prescribe a solution that allays those fears, sets a course for success, and ultimately delivers your client to that desirable future state where those fears and pains are no more.

It's not about shaming, coercing or bullying. It's about HELPING.

As part of your insight gathering, be sure to ask questions of your ideal-fit prospects that allow them to share their deepest fears. This may require some form of "warming up" or connection with the subject as these fears will often be very personal. They tend to be less about their business and more about their own plans, experiences and situation.

To ensure consistency and relevance, too, these fears should relate to the challenges they've already shared.

Once you feel that you've made the necessary connection and can comfortably delve into the more personal recesses of their minds, start by asking them the question "What's your biggest fear, should you have to continue without fixing these challenges?".

Responses might include things like:

- We may miss our growth goals for the coming year"
- "I'll likely be looked over for promotion or otherwise fail to progress in my role very quickly"
- "Not fixing these challenges may result in major cuts to department funding or even redundancies"

Again, adopt the Five Whys strategy to elicit the best and most impactful responses possible and dig deeper into the face-value responses you may otherwise generate.

3. Goals

On the right side of the matrix is where we determine where your prospect is looking to go in the future. What does the world look like where the challenges that they expressed to you earlier are completely eradicated and solved (ideally with your help)?

Paint a picture of a nirvana-like existence once they've removed these pains and unlocked the potential that exists beyond those obstacles.

This part of the process often comes a little easier to your prospect than speaking about the challenges and fears that they harbour in their business. Let's face it, it's a lot more pleasant to talk about the future potential and the positive aspects of your company's fortunes than to talk about the negatives.

In the Goals section of the matrix, we are primarily going to focus on the targets related to the company rather than the individual.

Responses gathered from prospects in this section tend to gravitate towards revenue and growth-based metrics. However, the more creatively minded prospects will be able to visualise a future that includes many other facets, such as cultural aspects of the team dynamic, recognition-based aspects like awards and accreditations and other elements that won't be related purely to the numbers.

It's a rarity that those in decision-making roles have not set goals for their department or company as a whole. But you would be amazed at the number of instances I've encountered over the past 12 years to suggest that the vast majority of respondents have some doubts or lack of clarity about what they're truly looking to achieve in the future. So, you may need to help them identify and extract the best possible responses that not only help them but also help you in understanding them at a sufficiently deep level.

Start by asking them the simple question "What are your goals for the company over the next 12 months and beyond?"

As before, let's use the Five Whys technique to get the most valuable responses. In challenging their goals with this method of questioning, you'll dive deeper into the real reasons those goals exist, why they arrived at certain numbers and how they are going to support other aspects of their business progression in the future.

Capture those goals and enter them into the top right box of the matrix before moving on to the Ambitions section.

4. Ambitions

Now we move back into personal territory. This is where individuals see themselves in this vivid future, now unshackled from the constraints of the challenges and obstacles that you've removed.

This is arguably the most compelling section of the matrix. We can all relate to the visualised future; the existence that we see for ourselves and strive for. We all set goals for ourselves every day, dreaming of a time when certain aspects of our lives are improved and we're ultimately much happier.

Of course, levels of ambition vary from one individual to the next. We should be mindful of this when questioning or challenging these ambitions. After all, some ambitions may have been harboured and nurtured for many years and are highly personal to the individual. Therefore, tread carefully when using the Five Whys technique.

Ask the question "What are your specific ambitions for the future and where do you see yourself after these challenges have been solved?"

Make sure that the responses you capture in this quadrant are relevant to the challenges, fears and goals you've captured before, and can adequately support you in forming a position that allows you to provide the best possible solution.

CLIENT STORY – Bright Frog

Bright Frog is a technology consultancy serving the healthcare sector. One of the many firms with a heavy focus on "digital transformation" as their lead service. It's the subject of all their messaging and positioning.

Here's the thing: at the time of writing (and likely still the case as you read this), there's no shortage of digital transformation specialists, consultancies and agencies out there. It's one of those zeitgeist terms (like cybersecurity) that dominates the business landscape and contributes to the "white noise" that permeates social media, email inboxes, and networking conversations worldwide.

In short, it's VERY MEH!

When challenged, Bright Frog identified that their best clients to date had approached them for help with project recovery. Many healthcare organisations had already embarked on some form of transformation but these projects were typically plagued with inefficiencies, near-terminal challenges, communication breakdowns and both time and cost overruns.

Bright Frog harboured a reticence to position the entire business around the project recovery solution, despite admitting that the size of market for this challenge would likely serve them with all the business they would ever need to meet their growth goals for the future.

When digging further into this deep-rooted concern, it transpired that project recovery proved, in many cases, to be a fantastic "entry programme" that opened the door to many of the complimentary solutions that Bright Frog offers. Lightbulb moment!

Armed with this insight, we were able to agree a plan to lead a segmented approach to positioning project recovery as one of a handful of solutions that Bright Frog could lead with. We agreed to create a hyper-targeted client acquisition journey around this one challenge to generate the demand in a far more focused way.

What's more, with the right measurement and reporting in place, we would be able to easily assess the efficacy of this approach versus their entire digital transformation proposition – an evidence-based marketing strategy that would serve them very well indeed without falling foul of a potential "all eggs, one basket" scenario.

A Different Belief

What do you stand for?

What do you stand against?

When it comes to creating a market position and appealing to the right profile of buyer, it's a very good thing to convey your core values and "stance" on certain aspects of business – especially the way it's conducted in your sector or business category.

But to have your stance land with a thud with your buyers, it's a good idea to take a polarising position: one that stands firmly opposite a widely held (and often wildly damaging) position, belief or way of doing business and that is employed by many of your competitors.

Why is it important to stand for or against something?

To put this in the context of the buyer's brain and the things that your prospects must see, hear and feel to be convinced that you're the best option for them, we are again triggering that "this is different" or "I've not seen/heard this before" element. To go against the grain and rally against the norm is one of the most effective and compelling ways to convey differentiation and to attract a buyer to your way of thinking.

This is especially effective in situations where the buyer has tried to fix a challenge before, perhaps with the help of a competing solution provider, and has come up short time and time again. In these circumstances, the buyer really needs to know that they are faced with a different path – and that begins with alignment on an alternative way of thinking.

By default, when you take a strong and vocal (visible) stance one way or another, it implies in the strongest terms that you stand alone – if not in the view itself, then in the amplification of your viewpoint.

In simple terms, if you're the one to shout loudest in your opposition or support of your stance – and the buyer agrees – you'll be the only one that matters in that buyer's mind.

Let's take a look at some examples:

Nike's support of Colin Kaepernick, the NFL player who first took the knee in protest at the treatment of Black people and people of colour in the US around 2016. There was well-publicised opposition to Nike's stance, with many customers burning their trainers (sneakers), often on camera and shared via social media, but the overwhelmingly positive impact on their brand image saw Nike add more than $6 billion to the com-pany's market value during that period.

Many, too, will remember the advertising campaign launched by HSBC in the wake of the Brexit vote here in the UK. Richard Ayoade proclaim-ing that "we are not an island" was seen by many as too provocative a claim and many were vocal in their disdain for the campaign and for the company. Ultimately, the resulting debate transcended television and brought the desired publicity to HSBC. Admittedly, and somewhat ironically, they lost a substantial amount of that goodwill by moving a great many jobs from the UK to France in the years that followed!

Your stance doesn't have to be on such a grand scale or cause out-cries among the general population but it should light at least a small fire in those you wish to influence – your buyers and partners.

One such stance that we adopt is to fly in the face of what has be-come common convention around "cold messaging". There are many, many marketing gurus and agencies out there, peddling the concept of mass outreach and automation, causing a cold email and follow-up deluge of biblical proportions. It's not just the email inboxes of the B2B world that are filling up but the LinkedIn inboxes, too. The "connect and pitch" strategy, where you're invited to connect on the basis of some tenuous and weak link before being pummelled with sales rhetoric and a "book a call" call-to-action, is alive and not so well.

It's lazy and, in my opinion, needs to stop.

So that's what I'm *against*. What am I *for*? Well, it's the opposite: a low volume, manual, highly-personalised approach to connecting with individuals online based on "warmer" actions and triggers that tell me in no uncertain terms that a dialogue is warranted and welcomed.

It won't reach thousands of people every week or month. It won't help me to "hyperscale". It won't position me as a "hustler", who wishes to be omnipresent online, seen and revered by all. Perish the thought. Instead, it's intended to sit better with my core values and recognise that my buyers are (deep down) also opposed to these intrusive and annoying techniques. It sits better with me and my core values and it just happens to resonate better with those I wish to influence.

You can go too far in adopting your polarised position, however. As with any business activity but especially in marketing, test everything! Validate your position with your target audience (the only people that really matter) to ensure they aren't offended. Check that they agree with the sentiment of your stance. Also, is it polarising enough that you're likely to set the cat amongst the pigeons with your views?

STEP 2:
Full Differentiation

People aren't overtly looking for "different" or at least they don't know they are.

So why is it so important?

In reality we've not evolved a great deal from the same humans that roamed the lands thousands of years ago that needed to easily spot the sabre-toothed tiger lurking in the long grass. In short, what stood out as different would quite often save our lives!

It's the same evolutionary trigger that determines whether your content, your ads, your website, or your spoken pitch earn and retain the attention you crave or is instead consigned to the "you had your chance and you blew it" drawer of obscurity by your otherwise would-be buyers.

Is full differentiation the same as a USP?

You're likely familiar with the concept of a Unique Selling Proposition (USP). In the quest for full differentiation, is this the same thing?

The unique part should be an aim, for sure. If you're unique, you are by definition, differentiated.

And a fully differentiated offer will help you not only to sell at higher volumes with less resistance but to attract more opportunities to do so. So the S of USP also gets a big tick.

Your position is also the lens through which your proposition is viewed by your ideal buyers, so the P lines up as well.

So, yes it is very similar but, as you'll learn in these pages, old language switches the buyer brain off. If I were to talk about USPs the whole time, I'd be lumping myself in with all manner of brand strategists and marketers, most likely peddling some decades-old process that doesn't reflect the ever-changing marketing landscape.

So in this section, we'll discuss three ways in which you can sufficiently differentiate yourself from others who might promise to deliver similar results, so you can swerve the pit of competitive pressure forever...

1. A different category

I'll show you how to achieve category ownership: the process of completely removing yourself from the crowd of competitors who label themselves in the same ways and unwittingly perpetuate a culture of competition.

This is where we first encounter the process of vocabulary transformation, to make your business "unpigeonholeable" – a vital step in reducing or completely obliterating price resistance. After all, if you can't be compared, how can buyers possibly put a price on what you do? We'll open up the possibility of a truly value-based sale – one which allows you to shake off the shackles of "competitive plus" pricing.

When deployed as part of your pitch and promotional materials, your new category language will pique intrigue and curiosity levels, commanding higher levels of attention and response.

2. A different mechanism

We'll craft or refine an existing mechanism or system for delivering the transformation you offer. Any buyer needs to have ultimate confidence that yours is a proven process; that they're not the latest guinea pig in your make-it-up-as-we-go-along programme.

Your unique mechanism will provide that confidence as well as a solid, tangible visual for use in your sales conversations and presentations. Not only that but your mechanism may even solidify your own staff's understanding of the value you provide as a business and unify everyone's voice on the matter of "what you do".

We've even had some of our clients complete this part of the journey and then totally revise their internal operational processes to reflect the upgrades we've created together.

3. A different language

By this point, you'll have used language transformation to take ownership of a new category but it needn't stop there. There are so many other aspects of your business vocabulary that we can lift and augment using this methodology.

From your solutions to buyer challenges to your people and marketing collateral, we'll leave no stone unturned for the many elements we can amplify with new wording, generating a stronger resonance and response with every potential buyer.

By the end of this process, you'll have everything you need to create your "Language Library": a hugely valuable resource that puts the icing on the differentiation cake.

Let's get into it, shall we?

A Different Category

We've been trained to use language that gives comfort and under-standing to others. In the age of Search Engine Optimisation (SEO), there's a certain amount of benefit in being discoverable for the search terms and keywords that our audience would use to describe us. There's "safety" in describing ourselves in the same way that our competitors would describe themselves and which places us firmly in a known category.

Prospects will thank you for referring to yourself with well-trodden language.

It's human nature to seek the comfort of a known entity. The mo-ment you tell somebody what you do, they will search the deepest and darkest recesses of their mind for a similar business or person they know that fits the same description or falls into the same category.

"Oh, you're a bit like..."

It can feel like this perception of familiarity and understanding is a good thing, working in your favour but there's also a great deal of baggage that comes with that understanding.

Whilst running my marketing agency, Influence Agents, I met count-less prospects and potential clients who found similar comfort in comparing us to other marketing agencies and consultancies they'd come across and used in the past.

Here are some of the assumptions they made, as a result of making that immediate comparison:

Nobody thinks these things without prior personal experience or having heard it from a trusted source. In short, they're bringing all the baggage of their previous dealings and their general understanding of your category and dumping it right on you before you even have the chance to educate them on your business and offering.

Not fair, is it?

The good news is that there's a way around it and it harnesses the power of language and perception to tick all of the checkboxes in the "buyer brain". Those same checkboxes that, when ticked, leave no legitimately great-fit client with a justifiable reason to reject you.

The first two checkboxes – feelings we need to elicit in our buyer – are:

1. "This is for me"
2. "I haven't seen/heard this anywhere else before"

The first is about relevance and attention. When seeing or hearing your messaging, whether in an email, a tweet, over the phone or in a face-to-face pitch, your prospect must feel that it's directed specifically at them.

You can do this in one of two ways. Either you speak to a very particular challenge that only your ideal buyer would be experiencing (made even better if you have an eventual solution to that challenge) or you specify the exact buyer type in your messaging, e.g. "We help London-based CTO's in the financial services sector…".

The second checkbox we must tick is about novelty and that's where establishing a NEW category can be a really good thing. Find a way to describe your business and its place in the world without using a known category name or well-trodden industry moniker and you'll switch the buyer's brain ON to whatever you say next.

Why does this work?

Well, I'm no anthropologist, but I do understand the "fight or flight" mechanism that's been firmly embedded in the human psyche since the dawn of man. We've long been programmed to take notice of what's different; it's what has kept us alert to the dangers associated with daily life, whether it's a bear in the wild or a speeding vehicle on the city streets.

In the world of business and marketing, difference is what gets us noticed. So, "different" is the basis of attention. And with attention being so in-demand and in such short supply, wherever you seek it, you would do well to harness whatever you can to make your business stand out to your prospective buyers.

What is a category anyway?

People don't tend to like to be pigeonholed, type cast or considered "one of many". It's boring. The concept of a category in business has been challenged and questioned more and more in recent times. The acceleration of new categories being born, first in Silicon Valley and latterly in startup hubs around the world, has given rise to a revolution of what I call "unpigeonholeable" companies.

The overly-cited examples are Uber and Airbnb, which birthed new sectors and business models in the worlds of transport and accommodation respectively.

Unpigeonholeable works. It achieves the novelty factor that massively ticks the buyer brain box of "I haven't seen or heard this before". We're not talking about category creation, as that would suggest a complete overhaul of your business model and value proposition. No, what I'm talking about is category ownership.

That's achievable even for companies that have been in business, adhering to established business practices, for many years. You can retrofit category ownership into any B2B company simply by dialling up the language associated with your brand and pitch.

When done right, this achieves similar status to that suggested by Renée Mauborgne and W. Chan Kim in their 2004 book "Blue Ocean Strategy", which has been cited and strived for by many ever since.

The implication is that many sectors or categories have produced a "red ocean": a market that is so saturated by competition that the waters have turned red with the blood of a shark-induced feeding frenzy. Red oceans may provide ultimate validation that there's demand for your services but they can get pretty tricky to navigate, as competitors position themselves ahead of you and compete on price. This may be sufficient to drive buyers to the lowest bidder, harming the category as a whole and commoditising your once highly valued services.

Instead, the "blue ocean" represents a new category. One that has no competitive pressure but still contains enough pent-up demand to fuel your growth goals for all time.

So, I want you to strive for category ownership.

By the end of this process, you'll be able to clearly and confidently complete the statement "We are the world's only...".

Let's now decide what follows that opening of the statement, to provide you with the ultimate pitch and the creation of a new category. A sparsely populated category with just one inhabitant... YOU!

Discoverability disclaimer

I mentioned earlier how we live in the age of SEO. That poses a challenge when it comes to the idea of category ownership and new language. Won't this harm our ability to get found online?

Great question. And it's important to recognise HOW we're going to be using this new language.

It's not about updating all your website headings, meta descriptions, image alt tags or anything else that might damage your discoverability by those searching for your newly-established category name via Google. After all... nobody will be searching for your category (yet)!

How you're found is one thing. What you tell the prospective buyers that find you is quite another. You still need to optimise your site so that you're found by the right people using established language and keywords – nothing changes from that perspective.

But when you're presenting to those visitors, you'll use your new language to describe your offer and to *update* their understanding of your category and the value you deliver.

OK, now that's dealt with, let's look at the process for determining your new category language.

How to establish a new category language

This is as creative as you need to be during the entire process of escaping MEH. It is largely a logical process that plays on the needs of the buyer but this part is where we must actively adopt a vocabulary that jars with the recipient's expectations.

It's going to help a great deal to have a thesaurus at hand (use the free resource at thesaurus.com), so that you can find synonyms and alternative phrases to support your efforts. If, like most of us, you're not an Oxbridge English graduate, you'll benefit from the ability to quickly generate new ideas.

Next up, pull together a team of colleagues and stakeholders or perhaps even friends and family, so that you can get a more rounded opinion on the category language you'll be introducing. It's important to consider many different angles and connotations to your new business vocabulary and involve those that have a deep understanding of your ideal buyer.

Salespeople, client success or customer service reps, support staff and any other customer-facing colleagues should be able to give you their well-informed take on how your suggestions are likely to land. They should be able to assess whether the keywords and phrases will generate the attention and response you're aiming for before you go out and prove it for yourself.

Side note: All this is something that I'd be happy to help you with. Just reach out to me via the "usual channels"!

Also, I want you to absolve yourself of the responsibility of going from "normal" language to perfect, novel, attention-grabbing language all in one fell swoop.

Instead, we're going to take a staged approach like this:

Step 1 – Capture the established, "white noise", well-trodden language that does indeed lump you in with every other provider in your space. This is usually the most often-used terminology by prospects and participants in your space.

With reference to my SEO comment earlier, this is usually also the terminology you wish to be FOUND for when ranking in search engines. With broad appeal and understanding comes demand. Your new category language won't be used as search engine fodder but instead will engage those that do indeed find you.

At each stage of the process, I'll use a real-world example to show the type of language that might be used…

Example: **Cybersecurity**

Step 2 – Think of a better alternative that's more niche and specific but which is probably being used by a good many others still. This typically occurs where a competing provider has attempted to differentiate themselves without steering too far from the path most travelled. They tend to incorporate elements of common terminology or have created a "break-away" group of providers or companies that identify with an alternative presence.

In this instance, and building on the example of cybersecurity, we unearthed a category that more and more companies in the space are identifying with and which they feel offers more specificity and separation from the norm...

Example: **Threat detection**

Step 3 – Think of an even better alternative, which might have been established by a handful in your industry but certainly has not been adopted by the masses. This sort of category usually comes from one pioneering business establishing a new category language but insufficient protection of the language has given rise to a few "copycats".

I'll speak of protection shortly. For now, let's find an example of that less-used, copycat language that's certainly an improvement on what came before but which isn't unique...

Example: **Threat intelligence**

Step 4 – Jump to a new category and language that isn't being used by anyone else. Google it. Has this category been claimed by anyone else out there on the web?

Here's where it's important to have a basic understanding of how to use search engines for such means. If you were to simply search for a term like threat intelligence, the result would comprise all web pages indexed that contain either word or a combination of both – and not necessarily used in conjunction with each other.

So, we need a phrase search. Simply put quotation marks around your chosen phrase, such as "threat intelligence" and you're now searching for web pages that contain that specific phrase in its entirety.

At the time of writing, there are more than nine million results for this phrase. Not exactly different or unique!

Ideally, you're seeking a category that has ZERO competition but you can usually get away with a phrase that has limited search results or those that only relate to out-of-context situations.

Example: **Exposure discovery**

One of our clients in the cybersecurity space, Locus Cyber, went through this process with our guidance and established a new category of **"threat immunity"**.

This phrase immediately triggered some questions about how legitimate it was to claim immunity in the context of cybersecurity. Of course, full immunity can't be claimed at all, but if we learned anything during the course of the COVID-19 pandemic, it's that full immunity is rarely achievable.

In this context, it's a lesson in how we can question the language we arrive at and create illegitimate barriers that prevent us from forward progress. On this occasion, we were able to quickly move forward, having established a position that I want you to remember, too...

Your overall positioning (and certainly your category language) isn't about making promises that you can't later back up and show proof of.

Remind yourself of the desired outcome here... ATTENTION!

You can explain the details later. For now, adopt a language that causes a "pattern interrupt" and gets the very best eyeballs on your content, paying attention in a big way.

Locus Cyber went on to protect their category language with a trademark, at least in their target locale, and whilst you'll find more mentions of the term online now, none are used in the same field or in a directly competitive way. Crucially, it remains THEIR language.

The category "Top 'n' Tail"

So, you have your new category but at this point it's likely lacking a couple of important aspects that will make it usable "in the field"...

Context and Entity.

Context

For your category to hit home with the desired target profile of buyer, we need to tell them WHO it's for. An easy way to do this is to add the niche, industry or function that you best serve and want to connect with.

Examples could include:

- Financial services (industry)
- Public sector (sector category)
- InsureTech (emerging category)
- Fulfilment (department or function)
- CTO/Chief Technology Officer (job title or role)
- Startup or Scaleup (stage of growth)

However you refer to your niche, it needs to make obvious (to the businesses within it) who you do your best work for. Ultimately, it has to invoke that feeling of "this is for me", which is the very basis of attention.

If you don't include a niche industry, category, role or similar, you must at least speak to a challenge that your ideal buyers would identify with. Again, this will resonate with your buyer, leaving them comforted that they are understood.

Only then can they even consider responding or identifying themselves as a prospect.

If we bolt the context or niche onto our category, we may end up with something like **"Exposure discovery for FinTech companies"**. We've incorporated our new language and conveyed the specific segment of buyer that we work with.

Remember, this is purely your position and pitch for one specific buyer and it can be replicated for many diverse buyer types and segments.

Entity

It's difficult to refer to your own business without including some sort of descriptive "entity".

The most commonly used entities include:

- Consultancy
- Agency
- Partners
- Associates

These examples demonstrate the MEH, ubiquitous language that we often adopt when describing our business.

But whilst we're striving for full differentiation and creating a new vocabulary for our category, why not do this for the entity too?

Explore some of the options below and consider firing up the thesaurus to build the ultimate category/entity combination:

- Pioneers
- Gamechangers
- Sherpas
- Gurus
- Fixers
- Pacesetters
- Magicians
- Technicians

Yes, yes, I know... many of these examples are a little "out there" and you may feel uncomfortable referring to yourselves as "magicians". However, it's more important what your target buyer thinks. Would they respond positively?

Your chosen entity and language in general, needs to match your desired tone. If you're dealing with a largely formal or "stuffy" audience, try to match that energy whilst still taking a fully differentiated position.

So here's your "out"...

If your category is unique enough AND you've niched or segmented well enough, you may be able to get away with a safer option like "consultancy" or "agency". The key is the response. Are you achieving that pattern interrupt and piquing curiosity to never-before-seen levels?

Of your context, category and entity combination, two out of three tends to be enough to help you stand apart from the crowd.

So, where are we at? Your full category language might now look something like this...

"Exposure Discovery Specialists to the FinTech industry"

Certainly different!

Once you've gotten this far, you may wish to consider some additional steps, to make the very best of your endeavours.

Prove it before you lose it

Everything you've done up to this point has made use of the discovery phase and outcomes from the research you did, to determine the challenges your ideal buyers are facing, relative to your offering.

But that's no guarantee that your newly-acquired language will definitely land with those buyers and compel them to respond.

So, you'd do well to test it, first.

Reaching out to those who represent your ideal buyer profile gives you the opportunity to gather honest feedback and gauge the levels of enthusiasm around your category.

Make sure they understand the process you're undertaking and the purpose of differentiation that underlies your aims. That way, you'll hear less of the "I don't get it" responses that help nobody.

Here are some good sources of validation to consider:

- Staff (beyond those involved in the language exercise)
- Existing clients
- Current prospects and those in sales conversations with you
- Partners and referrers
- First-line connections on LinkedIn
- Email subscribers
- Twitter and other social followers

Protect it

I touched on trademarking earlier and it warrants a bit more "airtime". During the vocabulary creation process, you'll discover several terms that could be protected and turned into highly valuable intellectual property for your company: everything from your category to solutions and product names – anything that you feel is truly unique and could help to separate you from others in your market.

At a basic level, if you feel you'd be upset or annoyed if a competitor started using YOUR language to engage clients who should be beating a path to your door instead of theirs... protect it!

This can give rise to all sorts of partnership and licensing options further down the road but, for now, it's just good practice to cement ownership of your newly created collateral.

So, what's next?

You've just completed a process of vocabulary creation that will serve you well in a later section of the book, where we adopt the same steps to spin up new ways to speak about your challenges, solutions and other aspects of business language.

Before we get there, let's look at a real-world example of category language making a huge difference...

CLIENT STORY – Future Foundry

Prior to our work with Future Foundry, they proudly referred to themselves as an "Innovation Service". On the face of it, this sounds like a perfectly specific, relevant and different category but the innovation consultancy space is incredibly competitive. With innovation also being perceived as a very broad discipline that is difficult to define for many, the importance of a stand-out proposition became obvious to the FF team.

Their desire for differentiation wasn't born out of poor results or the usual "pipeline pain", however. Future Foundry had enjoyed amazing first-year growth and it was blatantly clear that the sales end of the client acquisition journey was in great shape.

They were even doing some stellar marketing work, running regular events from which they could repurpose a whole suite of assets and content to share with their audience via social and email.

The team needed help in two areas. First, amplifying and strengthening the message so that it landed harder with the best-fit prospects at their events. And second, boosting the impact of their follow-ups, primarily through email but ideally incorporating some aspects of effective social selling, too.

Category ownership was a priority, as well. In this highly competitive space, they found themselves up against the big four consulting firms, as well as many boutique and specialist innovation consultancies.

Future Foundry harboured a desire to be bolder and to make more tangible what was essentially a traditional money-for-expertise model.

After they followed our process of MEHscapology, we collectively landed on the "Corporate Innovation Engine". This encapsulated the market identity (organisations that recognised themselves as occupying the "corporate" bracket – a great filter for small businesses without the budget for the highest-level expertise) alongside what was intentionally positioned as packaged product language: the Innovation Engine. It's a very different entity to claim and the resulting expectation is one of more tangibility and certainty than a "service" or "consultancy" would conjure.

Future Foundry has continued to thrive and grow under their newly-positioned banner and I'm told that recent pitches have garnered a far more enthusiastic response than before the exercise. That's what we like to hear!

A Different Mechanism

An essential part of positioning your solution in the highest echelons of attraction is your Unique Mechanism (UM): the proprietary process by which you deliver transformation for your clients.

Every business delivers a transformation of sorts and this is no more prevalent than in the professional services industry. The expertise, guidance and systems that you provide allow for the resolution of a substantial challenge that your clients faced before they met you. The "before and after" is stark and the results are significant. Otherwise, why would you exist, let alone succeed?

The Unique Mechanism gives tangibility to any service offering. It's a way of packaging your process into a defined and methodical approach, showing your prospects the journey they can expect to take with you if their woes are to be consigned to history.

Not only will this provide an incredible sales asset, capable of aiding your prospective buyers in "getting it" in an instant but a well-defined and visual UM can also cement your internal understanding of the transformation process. This will help create repeatable and consistent systems for delivery. The client experience is elevated, social proof abounds and you may just see your NPS (net promoter score) soar, too.

So, why do you need a UM?

At last count, there are approximately 64,000 Microsoft Partners in the network, globally. Given that Microsoft offers a limited number of products via their partners, it's fair to say that there will be many thousands of consultancies and managed service providers, all offering the same solutions to their clients. Office 365, Power BI, SharePoint... How can you possibly differentiate your solutions when you're competing with tens of thousands of other providers?

The answer? A <u>UNIQUE</u> Mechanism allows them all to survive and thrive. Almost every provider offers a very different experience.

The *process* that you adopt even to install a popular, "carbon copy" solution into your client's business will be completely distinct from any other. You may not have defined this process as well as it needs to be if you want to gain and retain the attention of your highest-value prospects – but that's what this chapter is all about!

However competitive the space you operate in, get ready to completely differentiate your solutions, beginning with a structured, repeatable and visually appealing UM.

How to build YOUR Unique Mechanism

As with any effort when you start to revamp or transform your positioning or work on any marketing or sales effort, keep your exact target buyer in mind. Unless you conjure this deep understanding of your buyer, you may devise a UM that fails to resonate or inspire and presents a solution founded on crumbling foundations.

Your UM can be linear (typically for one-off, project-based solutions) or cyclical (better for the ongoing, retainer-based engagements that managed and professional services providers prefer). It could even be a combination of the two, with an initial, linear transformation continuing to a cyclical delivery or maintenance service. Choose the model that best suits your solution before proceeding with this simple process:

Step 1 – The RESULT (Future)

Start with the end in mind. Visualisation is a powerful tool in many aspects of business. Use it now to create a vivid image of the future that your ideal buyer wants to create. I like to ask a very simple question when seeking to learn the desired outcome from a potential client:

"Let's imagine you and I are sitting down over coffee a year from now. We're reflecting on what a fantastically successful year it's been; one where you've achieved every goal you set for yourself representing significant growth both for the business and for you. What's happened in that time?"

The answer to this question should unlock a varied and valuable mine of insights about the individual's deepest desires. It could also uncover desired outcomes/metrics related to their situation, such as:

- Revenue growth
- Number of clients
- Lead generation and marketing results
- "Hats" they are wearing (and no longer wearing) in the business, allowing them to do their best work and "take a step back" from activities they don't enjoy
- Recruitment and team makeup
- Personal life – their own income, time (and quality of time) with family or on passion projects
- Their perfect technology stack and supporting infrastructure

One individual is fine but if you repeat this enough times, you'll gain an overarching understanding of entire market segments and "personas" that will serve you for a long time. After all, even in this fast-paced world in which we live, human behaviour still takes an incredibly long time to change. The psychological triggers in the "buyer brain" will remain relatively constant, long enough for you to work your magic and grow your own business to new heights.

Got a thorough understanding of the RESULT your prospects wish to achieve? Check!

Step 2 – The REALITY (Now)

Now that you've got your prospect excited at the thought of targets being hit and a more enjoyable existence a year from now, we need to bring them crashing back down to reality and discuss where they're at right now.

The reason for taking the wind abruptly from their newly-filled sails? Well, we need to establish what many marketers call "The Gap". It's the distance between where they are now and where they want to be. As before, we want to get into the guts of the buyer's experience, putting a stark focus on the challenges and frustrations they experience every day. Why are they not already enjoying the attractions and rewards of a successful business? Why do they have to wait until next year? Why are they doubting that the results you discussed are even achievable?

It's important to recognise any successes that your prospect has achieved to date. Taking a judgmental position may create an overtly-crushing sense of disappointment and failure that's difficult to recover from. Keep a balanced air of optimism and anticipation and show that the formula for success is right around the corner.

As with the first step, we want to establish some key factors and metrics around their current reality, relative to your solutions. They might include:

- What's their monthly/annual revenue now?
- What does their team and state of recruitment look like?
- What does their current tech stack look like, and what's missing?
- Why do they think they are where they are?
- What are they doing right now to attempt to fix the situation or correct the course?
- How's that working out for them?
- What would happen if they didn't achieve their goals or resolve a serious challenge in their business within a certain timeframe?
- What needs to change?

Note that the tone of these markers is somewhat different to the Result step. There's more emphasis on what they've attempted and highlighting the absence of success with that path, making the need for change even starker.

Gathering these insights from a number of clients, prospects and "friendlies" will help you cement your understanding of the methods that simply haven't worked within your target audience. It will also highlight the deep frustrations and headaches ensuing from the "merry-go-round" that many will feel they're still firmly on.

Time to bring the energy down even further!

Step 3 – The ROADBLOCKS (Obstacles)

OK, so we've established that the buyer has some solid and compelling goals that they wish to achieve. And we've established that there are some telling factors at play preventing them from achieving them. We've identified "The Gap", stretched it a little to make it seem more pressing and real, and agitated the pain to new heights.

Given that many buyers will have had many attempts at fixing this situation before, it's fair to assume that they've likely encountered a few roadblocks along their journey. To better position your solution and to ensure that you account for these hurdles you need to first identify them all.

Ask what is already blocking them and what might jump out and stop them from reaching that oh-so-attractive destination in 12 months' time. Some of those roadblocks may include:

- Lack of vision
- Lack of plan or strategy
- Lack of skills or skilled talent
- Environmental or economic issues
- Absence of tools, software or infrastructure
- Mindset
- Budget
- Toxic culture
- The inability to make swift/agile decisions

You will already be ahead of many competing advisors and solutions providers if you can simply account for the "unknowns" and communicate a more proactive approach to heading off anything that would derail the client's path to success. Capture the most commonly-occurring roadblocks (picture a wall that stands between your buyer's current reality and desired destination) and you can start to plot the steps, tools and waymarkers that get them past those stumbling blocks with ease.

Step 4 – The ROUTE

Steps one to three have been about creating a solid footing on which to build your UM. The Route is your proprietary process or system that helps your clients to traverse the usual obstacles on their path to success in a better-defined, more tangible and visible way.

The mechanism is the journey and the steps along the way to get your clients over the hurdles; to arrive at their desired future state without the pains and inconveniences that might accompany an alternative route (more on the essential process of "invalidation" later).

Each step should build on the last to move them away from the painful current reality to that nirvana-like future existence. They are the stepping stones to success but how do we identify them?

In his excellent book, Built to Sell (possibly the most well-thumbed in my modest collection), John Warrillow argues the case for your Unique Mechanism to be used as a sales tool – a visual representation of the delivery or transformation process that delivers a more solid punch than any verbal persuasion could ever muster.

We've used this framework in much the same way. Buyers love the clarity it brings to the delivery process and the solidity it offers to an otherwise intangible proposition.

Step 5 – The VALIDATION

Your Unique Mechanism may fall down in one or two key areas.

Firstly if you leave gaps in the process: the stages of your unique mechanism fail to account for one of the challenges/pains that your buyer is experiencing, one of the goals or ambitions that they've identified as important to their future or one of the obstacles they see as potentially standing in their way.

Secondly, you may have one or more stages in your process that are superfluous to requirements and fail to solve any of the challenges, goals or obstacles presented. If no legitimate buyer requirements are accounted for by that stage, does it need to be included? This could be an opportunity to simplify your process and ultimately give yourself and your team less work to do in the delivery of the transformation to the client.

How to validate:

1. Number your stages one to five or however many stages you've identified for your UM.

2. One by one, go through the challenges, goals and obstacles captured and mark them with the number of the stage that solves that requirement. For example, if one of the pains or challenges is solved by stage three of your UM, mark it with the number three.

3. Repeat this for all client requirements and look for any gaps. Do any remain unaccounted for by any stage of the mechanism? If so, consider adding a stage that solves this challenge, goal or obstacle. This may also be a good time to consider whether any unchecked requirements are legitimate concerns.

4. Take a look at the numbers you've attached to each requirement. Does any stage fail to tick off any of the stated requirements? You may want to ditch that stage and simplify your process, perhaps reducing the number of stages from five to four, for example.

Once you're happy that your UM is validated, it's time to name it!

Step 6 – The IDENTITY

Once your UM is ready to go, it's time to think about what to call it. This is an important step as the name you choose will become the identity of your solution. It has the potential to become synonymous with your business and brand, so it's worth taking some time to brainstorm a few different options before narrowing it down to the one that best represents your product.

Keep in mind that, much like the mechanism itself, the name should be unique, easy to remember and reflective of the solution's key benefits. With a little creativity, you can come up with a name that perfectly captures the essence of your UM and creates elevated levels of curiosity amongst your target market.

CLIENT STORY – Waymark

Prior to their adventure with TGO, Waymark positioned themselves as providing "software development services for organisations". This was generic on both challenge and segment in one of the most competitive sectors on earth!

They had a great sales track record, thanks to their deep expertise and high quality of service and client success but felt they needed a way to "lift" the message. Attention is at a premium in the digital sector and that first hit of information can make the difference between a solid enquiry or a hard pass.

The Waymark team were enthused at the opportunity to create a Unique Mechanism that encapsulated their proven delivery system and communicated the many tools that they deploy at various stages of their engagements. This would bring consistency and ultimate accuracy to everything that they do.

The "XITE framework" (spelling out the stages eXplore, Ideate, Transform, Evolve) that ensued not only gave them a hugely powerful asset to deploy in their marketing, pitching and sales but also caused them to rethink their internal delivery processes. Waymark saw an opportunity to further fine-tune their approach and ensure that what they sold was also what they delivered, every time.

The team has deployed this mechanism countless times since our work together closing some impressively sizeable projects along the way. It's a real testament to their ambition levels and refusal to accept the status quo.

A Different Language

Earlier, we took a sledgehammer to your category language and turned you into the "World's only..." in your chosen area of specialism. We upgraded the words you use and the perception you create for your business.

But there are many more elements to your business and communications that would benefit from a "language lift". If we're to do ultimate justice to your positioning and ability to pitch any perfect-fit client, we need to give your company's vocabulary the full works.

Here are a few more business entities and assets that we'll inject with some curiosity-causing wording:

- **Challenges** – the way we refer to the pains and success blockers that your buyers are experiencing.
- **Solutions** – does the positioning and naming of your products and services put them in the best possible light?
- **People** – there are many different players in your business success, including your staff, clients, partners, other stakeholders and even competitors. Giving each of them an identity provides an opportunity to stand even further apart from the norm.
- **Marketing assets and sales collateral** – positioning your lead magnets, events, brochures and other collateral will make it even more appealing to the right buyers, lifting conversion rates and eradicating MEH in your top-of-funnel activities.

- **Meetings and calls/appointments** – prospects have had enough of the lazy call and appointment offers. Nobody wakes up thinking "I want to sign up for a strategy session today!", let alone an "informal chat". Giving an identity to each meeting should further entice engagement and response in the right people.

As we get deeper into this exercise, I'll provide you with some examples of the "white noise", ubiquitous wording that many use before repeating the "less bad → better → best" process to achieve an unME-Hlievable vocabulary (sorry!).

Let's remind ourselves why we're doing this, shall we?

Language creates perception. If you use the same or similar language to your competitors in your messaging (email, social media, etc.), headlines, calls to action, and anywhere that your marketing or sales process meets the prospect, you'll be equated directly with them.

That could bring a whole heap of baggage that you really don't need.

Your buyers may have had varied experiences working with other providers in your space or heard horror stories about contacts and colleagues who have fallen foul of a less-than-perfect competitor. Your category language and your wider marketing vocabulary can create a perception of parity with the ne'er-do-wells of your industry – or help to set you apart.

Language *is* perception.

You can choose to perpetuate a perception of parity (say that five times fast!) or flip the script, re-write your own company dictionary and change the perception of your buyers, so that any effort to compare becomes folly.

That's the power of language and its effect on the "buyer brain". It has the power to pique attention and curiosity in those you want to attract, whilst filtering OUT those that you've no interest in working with. Your words will help you stand apart from the ever-increasing noise that permeates both the online and offline worlds, so that you can reach those buyers with a laser-like focus.

Some good news for you, now. The process we're going to follow to establish your language in each of those entity areas is the same as that used for your revamped category, with a tiny bit of research and data-gathering bolted onto the front end.

The list above is not exhaustive but you'll likely have identified a few assets in your business that can be subjected to the "language lift" treatment.

With that in mind, let's get started!

Step 1 – build a list of assets that require some uplift by scouring your "resource library", shared drives, filing cabinets, handbag... you get the idea. A resource library is a collection of useful and relevant assets that can help move prospects and clients forward in their challenge; content that boosts your credibility and position as help-ful adviser.

Leave no stone unturned and don't discount anything that you think might not be good or irrelevant enough. Many people have firm views on which assets are marketing related and which aren't – but they're not always correct.

Almost any business content you create has the potential to be a marketing asset. Even the internal-facing content that's intended for colleagues and other stakeholders can improve your collective un-derstanding as a team of the market, your proposition and your value to the client.

An example list could look something like this, taken from our own business model here at TGO:

1. Challenge – Companies with a website, pitch, wider messaging and marketing materials that make them look and sound like everybody else in their industry.

2. Challenge – Reaching out to potential prospects via email, LinkedIn and phone only to get ghosted or otherwise generate no response.

3. Challenge – Content is dull and fails to inspire prospects to connect and enquire with any regularity.

4. Solution – Achieve differentiation and build an un-turn-downable offer that prospects feel foolish to ignore or reject.

5. People – A team of specialist positioning consultants, experienced in helping companies achieve full differentiation and top-tier positioning.

6. Marketing or sales collateral – An evaluation or diagnostic "quiz" that helps prospects establish just how poor their current positioning is and shows them the potential for improvement.

7. Meeting or call – A triage call that assesses the requirements and fit between us and a prospective client.

8. Meeting or call – A subsequent "strategy" call that establishes specific goals and provides a high-level positioning strategy and further clarity on how we might work together.

Once you have a list and are struggling to add any more items to it, pull your creative, client-facing "brain trust" together once more and get started on the vocab transformation process.

Step 2 – Repeat·the White noise → Less Bad → Better → Best process of creating unique examples for your new language across each of the entity types that you've chosen to refresh.

As an example, let's take my company's first challenge: that of companies having a website, marketing messaging, etc. that looks and sounds like others in their space.

Old, "white noise" language = **Undifferentiated business**

Less bad = **Carbon copy marketing**

Better = **Twinning**

Best = **Same-ism**

Step 3 – Validate internally and jump onto Google to prove the digital tumbleweeds ... zero (or close to zero) results for your new vocabulary.

Remember, the results of this exercise will be subjective and will rely on the collective agreement of your brain trust. Sense check with the group whilst fully owning the identity of your ideal buyer. After all, it's their "lens" through which your proposition will be viewed.

Ask yourself, "would our ideal client feel that this represents new language, creating the necessary levels of intrigue and attention we desire?"

If the answer is a solid YES, you're onto a winner or at least a "Version 1.0" that you can validate with actual clients, prospects and "friendlies" in your target market.

Step 4 – Validate externally: test in earnest with those that represent your target buyers, as described in the Category Ownership section.

You can then start thinking about the outputs: the places and assets where this new vocabulary needs to permeate to have the greatest impact on your audience. Typically, this means voicing your new language wherever your business meets your audience...

- Website
- Email signatures
- Social profiles, bios and headers
- Advertising copy
- Banners and print materials
- Webinar and presentation decks
- Scripts and sales collateral
- Google Business Profile and other online directories
- Partner websites (where your bio and services may be listed)

I'll provide some further guidance on how to get the most from this "position activation" phase later in the book.

For now, we're done with creating a different language, and claiming full differentiation for your business. Let's complete the transformation by crafting an un-turn-downable offer and ticking those remaining checkboxes in the "buyer brain" – after we check out another client story.

CLIENT STORY – Project 4 Learning Lab

As always, we look at the "before" shot first. Positioned as an accelerator of learning for organisations, Project 4 Learning Lab (P4LL) is an already-successful consultancy. It works with some of the largest and best-known organisations in the world, helping them to deliver physical products to market more efficiently.

They specialise in the agile methodology for improving productivity and cost efficiencies in complex projects, which in their case appeals to project and programme managers. The only problem was that it wasn't at all obvious from their website or other digital properties that this was their greatest superpower. So step one was to bring that proposition to the forefront of their positioning.

The next task was to appeal only to those that required their help; those that feared the cost and time overruns on their programmes – a huge risk to reputation and credibility – in a way that allowed P4LL to swerve comparisons with the MANY other consultancies promising to turn around these failing types of programmes.

In this category, it's so easy to default to the type of overused terminology and jargon that lumps you in with the competition. The language library was a hugely important focus area for P4LL. Whether speaking about the people, their challenges, the potential solutions or the marketing assets deployed in their business, everything needed to support their new found desire to be different.

A range of new phrases resulted, forming an entire vocabulary that now allows the team to retain the interest and attention of their buyers throughout the buyer journey – not just at the initial connection. Terms like "flow fog", "agile apathy" and "assumption avalanche" won't mean much to the uninitiated – and that's intentional. But they support the arguments that P4LL make to their highly-targeted and specific audience.

At a trade show that followed just days after our work together, P4LL used this new language to book meetings with several "household name" prospects, who were full of praise for the differentiation displayed in their approach.

STEP 3:
An Un-Turn-Downable Offer

I t's a sad fact of business life that you don't win every deal that you would legitimately want to win.

Perhaps you've experienced this or something like it: prospects enter the sales process with you, show enthusiasm and are willing to exchange ideas. They extract value from the conversation but ultimately choose not to "exit via the gift shop".

In other words, they're escaping through the fire door, dodging anyone that might convince them to part with their hard-earned moolah!

The most frustrating part of this is that, in nine out of every ten cases I come across, the seller has a fantastic product or service and a killer track record of delivering results for their clients. They have a solid process for delivery and are set up with the people, resources and systems necessary to scale further. Their *only* problem is the absence of more great-fit clients for whom they can prove their incredible worth.

In the vast majority of cases, too, the prospect shows every sign of being highly engaged at every stage of the buyer journey. They appear to be in need of a solution like yours and have the power and budget to make the decision to work with you.

So, why do so many prospects duck out of the conversation before they can receive the value you promise?

- They didn't identify themselves as a great fit for your offering. The message didn't resonate, it wasn't specific enough for them to respond "this is for me" or the social proof examples given just didn't look like them.

- Perhaps the challenge that you spoke to wasn't the challenge currently bothering them the most or your description of it didn't tally with their understanding of it.

- It wasn't obvious what they could expect to get out of the process – the quantifiable result.

- Perhaps the timescale for an outcome was too long, or required a commitment beyond their comfort levels.

- They weren't convinced that your process or mechanism for delivery was effective or proven enough to generate a legitimate solution to their challenge.

- Your solution didn't appear to be superior to others on offer by competitors, or the experience seemed more laborious or friction-laden.

- The risk was too high – the potential failure to deliver a result wasn't sufficiently mitigated or risk wasn't shared proportionately on both sides. You failed to remove the perception of risk with a guarantee or performance/success-based condition.

- You sounded like a carbon-copy solutions provider, using the same old patter and language that lumps you in with the crowd of other available options.

What is an un-turn-downable offer?

I'm guessing that more than a few of you will have some doubts about the reality of the claim of an un-turn-downable offer. Can any offer from a business really be impossible to turn down?

Yes, it can but with some very stringent conditions attached. If you present your offer, proposal or pitch to a potential client, and don't receive the desired result, it may be due to one or more of the following causes:

- A sub-optimal value proposition
- A poorly-defined ideal buyer or a generic, broad-brush appeal
- The absence of an obvious and attractive outcome or "quantifiable result"
- The absence of a proven process or "unique mechanism" for delivery of the transformation on offer
- A perceived excessive (and possibly lopsided) risk in the deal
- The presence of competing solutions, which have not been adequately invalidated or disqualified as viable alternatives
- Dull, "white noise" language and messaging used to describe the proposition and your company
- Inconsistencies in the deployment of your proposition across marketing and sales channels

The combination of the targeting and differentiation steps we've covered, alongside the following section, will ensure that you account for all these requirements and more. This will provide the best chance of crafting an offer that is, indeed, un-turn-downable.

If you execute these steps to the letter, activate your position consistently across all channels you choose to exploit and still get turned down, chances are you're pitching to a maniacal self-saboteur, the likes of which you really didn't want to be working with anyway!

As I've mentioned more than a few times, your positioning provides the "lens" through which your target audience views your value proposition. It adds clarity and specificity, ensuring its radiant glow and vivid colours can be seen only by those to whom it should rightfully appeal.

Your "offer", in this context, is the detailed, client-facing version of your value proposition. You might think of it as a pitch but it is better structured to account for the needs present in the mind of your specific buyer.

Many refused offers are due to the mishandling of the value proposition creation process. Are you speaking to a legitimate, proven and validated need? Have you properly understood the pains experienced, the desired gains and the jobs undertaken by your best buyers?

Your offer will bring together all of the component parts you've built in the previous sections, along with three new elements (outlined below) that are guaranteed to elevate your pitch to new heights and convert a great many more opportunities into sales.

When do you know you've nailed it?

Results will vary and you can expect to see the fruits of your positioning labours in several ways. But most prevalent of all will be the conversion and "win" rates that you will enjoy, post-refresh.

That raises another area of deficiency that I see in many B2B organisations today: reporting and attribution.

We polled more than a hundred business owners and senior marketers/sales people, who identified positioning and earning the attention of prospects as their leading challenges. However, only slightly behind that was identifying and reporting on their own performance and return on marketing investment.

So, here's a very quick and simple process for measuring the impact of your positioning (and broader marketing) efforts:

1. **Identify the most important metrics**

   There are a heap of metrics and data points that you could measure across the full analytical landscape but your success really depends on a handful of them. Focus on the LAPS metrics: Leads, Appointments, Proposals (or presentations) and Sales.

2. **Benchmark where you're at right now through the client acquisition journey**

   Have a look at your past performance, relying on whatever data you can put your hands on, and capture the current state of play. How many leads do you generate per month on average, for example? How many of those leads progress to book appointments with you or take whatever action best represents this stage of your *sales* process?

   Complete the picture to include your proposals and sales (or their equivalents in your business) and you have your snapshot.

3. **Monitor the impact of your revised positioning, as you roll out your upgraded approach to marketing and sales**

   Continue to monitor these numbers and consider making the process part of your regular meeting schedule, so that you review performance over time.

   If you're not yet using a CRM (Customer Relationship Management) system or fancy marketing automation software, you can start by spinning up a simple spreadsheet to track these numbers.

As I mentioned in the introduction to this book, the effects of your positioning compound throughout the buyer journey.

Once deployed, your offer can help you to improve reach, response and click-through rates, lead generation, appointments booked, sales and retention. As you become more familiar with the process of position activation, you can start to get more sophisticated in your reporting and strategic marketing, to help "turn the right dials" to produce the commercial outcomes you desire.

For now, let's get some basic reporting in place, take a snapshot and embark on the final stage of our MEHscapology journey: building your un-turn-downable offer!

A Different Experience

Contrary to popular belief, you're *not* leaving money on the table.

Unless you're a pawnbroker or black-market arms dealer, it's highly unlikely that the money even made it to the table. But large swathes of the revenue that could be coming your way is still sitting rather comfortably in the bank accounts of your would-be clients. And you should consider that a big problem.

There's a required but oft-overlooked step when it comes to sales: the need to invalidate ALL other options your prospect has to solve their greatest and most painful-to-experience challenges.

You see, whilst other options remain in the mind of the buyer, as potential routes to take and solutions to buy into, there remains the possibility that you'll lose out. In short, if it's not a bloody obvious YES, then it could always be a no!

Your job and key takeaway from this section is to acknowledge and account for the many alternative paths that stand before your client-in-waiting and, one by one, close them off as viable solutions. The goal is to invalidate every competing path so that we leave yours as the only true, viable method for achieving a successful outcome.

What's it worth to your business?

Do you recall the ROI calculator from the Position and Pipeline section? Using that tool, we can easily determine the lifetime value of every deal you win or lose.

Based on the work we have done at TGO with consultancy and service provider clients (and without naming names), we consistently see the average deal value is well into six figures and often much higher. We're talking about high-impact and high-value projects and engagements that could set the tone for a working relationship that lasts for many years. Each of these deals contributes hugely to the growth of the client businesses and the personal ambitions and achievements of the leaders and staff that work for them.

Can you afford to lose deals of this magnitude for the sake of some very simple objection-handling and persuasion?

Let's look at who might be providing those competing solutions, based on a real-world scenario. Imagine you're a "digital transformation consultancy" looking to do business with companies in the healthcare sector.

You've been through the discovery phase and determined their most prevalent challenge:

- **Lack of clear digital strategy** – meaning a mix of new and outdated devices, a disparate range of (often unsupported) software products, varying degrees of virus and malware protection and a serious negative impact on productivity.

We could go much deeper into the impact of those factors on the wider business but that's enough information for us to explore some of the ways in which the prospect could resolve the problem or pain point…

Option #1
Partner with a managed service provider or IT support company

There are plenty of independent IT support companies and managed service providers that can swoop in with an assessment of the client's needs and prescribe technology solutions (hardware and software) to address the key challenges, maintain equipment, protect staff and their data and drive the digital direction of the business.

Option #2
Partner with a "Big Four" consultancy

If you're in consulting, you'll know these guys. Their names often complete the statement "Nobody ever got fired for hiring...", and include PwC, Deloitte, EY and KPMG (big fans of initialism). They're perceived as a steady hand and their reputations are often used to justify larger budgets.

Option #3
Partner with a direct competitor – in this case, a specialist digital transformation consultancy

These are typically the companies you're most keen to separate yourself from and look and sound less like when attempting differentiation. They're the companies that you may find yourself in a competitive situation against, whether by tender or direct engagement. If you've done any competitive analysis on your sector, these again will be well known to you.

Option #4
Hire an in-house IT director or manager

You may already be thinking that some of these options are folly for anyone that's looking to do a decent job of achieving their desired outcome.

Before we get to the invalidation process, however, we need to accept the fact that some prospects might see hiring and building an in-house capability as a solid and attractive option. In this instance, it could be an IT director or manager, a CTO or similar.

Option #5
DIY – manage the transformation and create a strategy themselves

We're onto the first of two options that many of you will need to invalidate in every opportunity: the DIY option. Depending on the complexity of your offering, you may encounter some chancer that thinks he has what it takes to swerve the expert assistance and get the job done "on the cheap".

Option #6
Do nothing

Lastly, there's the ever-present and uber-attractive option of just do-ing nothing. We are human beings after all; we live in the Deliveroo and Netflix age, where everything comes to us and the path of least resistance reigns supreme. We must invalidate the path whereby the prospect goes away to "think about it" and, in fact just continues to live with the challenge unresolved.

When this does happen, inevitably there's an absence of belief or trust in your solution, so you'll need to review other factors in your un-turn-downable offer and positioning.

Before we get into the process for creating invalidation statements, there's one ground rule that's worth calling out: this is NOT a smear campaign.

There's a reason why all of the examples above are framed as categories or profiles of supplier rather than a named company. You'd be well-ad-vised to adopt the same approach when completing this process for your company and proposition. This will ensure that you stick with the facts, maintain credibility and offer legitimate reasons why any category of solution is a truly bad idea without resorting to hearsay or conjecture.

OK, public service announcement out of the way. Let's get into it!

The process of invalidation

As with previous steps in the MEHscapology system, there's a simple process for determining the most powerful and appropriate invalida-tion statements for any pesky competing solution:

Step 1 – Identify competing solutions (not just direct competitors, but any method for solving the core challenge), listing them alongside the options of DIY and Do Nothing, as in the above example.

Step 2 – Research each competing solution to identify the differentiat-ing factors that separate their offering from yours. These could include:

- **Niche or specific client sector focus** – Are they positioned as specific enough to be able to deeply understand and serve the same buyer profile as you're targeting? A telling sign would be a landing page on their website that speaks to that particular sector or buyer profile.

- **Experience and social proof** – Has the competing provider published testimonials and case studies to promote and leverage the successes they've had with clients? Again, specificity wins, so how closely do those providing the social proof resemble the target buyer?

- **Unique Mechanism or proven process for delivering transformation to their clients** – Do they demonstrate a consistent, repeatable, and effective process for delivering transformation? Does it tick all the boxes that your solution does or are there key omissions that you can exploit via your invalidation statements?

- **A quantifiable result that forms part of their promise** – Does the alternative option present a tangible or quantifiable (metric-improving) result, within a meaningful timescale (ideally inside 90 days)?

- **Risk reduction or removal strategies, such as guarantees or performance-based deals** – How do competing providers mitigate perceived risk in the deal? Do they offer guarantees for any deliverable, phase or package of work, that would strengthen their sales argument?

- **General language, branding and tone of voice** – Is the competing solution presented using language that creates intrigue and excitement or with well-trodden, "white noise" vocabulary that lumps the provider in with the various other options in the category?

Capture all the notes you can – as exhaustive a list as possible, to inform the next step...

Step 3 – Craft compelling invalidation statements for each factor identified.

Invalidation statements make obvious to clients the reasons why a competing solution is unlikely to deliver the desired result.

Think about how a solution might fail or be otherwise inefficient, labour-intensive, costly or time-sapping. Consider all the things that could result in your prospect arriving squarely back at their current position again but many moons and many pounds/dollars/euros/Bitcoins later.

As before, I'm going to list some examples below, relative to the alternative options identified for the digital transformation consultancy proposition:

MSP or IT support company

- Not traditionally strategic in their thinking.
- Not vendor-agnostic. Often partnered with, and locked into deals with specific vendors, meaning you won't necessarily get the best solution.
- Offers no guarantee or obvious risk removal strategy – failure is possible without consequence.

Side note: If you're reading this and you're a managed service provider, cover off these potential objections in the buyer's mind before using variations on the invalidation statements for the below competing solutions.

"Big Four" consultancy

- Far from the most cost-effective option.

- The potential for hand-off to a junior, more inexperienced consultant, once the senior staff member has sold you the proposition.

- A rigid approach that's inflexible to your specific needs and is generic enough to apply across industries and business types.

Digital transformation consultancy

- No sector-specific experience or social proof. Do they really understand your sector and its challenges?

- Often bring in associates "off the bench" to run complex projects without the benefit of true integration with the wider team creating a disjointed experience.

- No risk-removal strategy or guarantee in place.

In-house IT director/manager/CTO

- Takes huge amounts of time and effort to attract and filter through candidates before selection.

- Huge costs associated with employment and training.

- Time-to-results can often be many months.

- The needs of the business are often front-loaded, meaning utilisation is low and wastage high after the initial strategy is deployed.

DIY

- Lack of experience and knowledge: more time taken to deliver a poorer outcome.

- Diversion of resource away from key initiatives in the business. Do you really have the capacity to support a complex programme like this?

- Low likelihood of delivering a compliant solution that meets industry standards.

Do nothing

- Continue to suffer the pains and challenges associated with not fixing this problem.

- Risk to reputation and employer brand. Will clients and staff wish to be associated with an organisation that doesn't deal with its problems?

- Competitive disadvantage. You'll be falling behind others in the sector until you solve this issue.

Repeat the process for all competing solutions, so you end up with an exhaustive list of reasons why each option is a HUGE no-no for potential clients.

With each invalidation statement, ask yourself the question "Can we quantify this in some way?".

Being able to attach a vital metric to the problem will further agitate the pain, helping it to land harder with the prospect and compel them more persuasively to take action.

Step 4 – Identify the three most compelling invalidation statements for use in your own offer, later. This can form part of your pitch and help out during the sales process to account for any remaining doubts or objections that may arise.

Your "trimmed" selection should be powerful enough first to attract the necessary levels of attention through intrigue and curiosity, and then applicable enough for as many of the competing paths as possible. Any statements that apply to many or all alternatives should be given more consideration for use in your formal pitch.

Portrait of a Groundhog

If we're ultimately to move the prospect to a place of action, any effort to invalidate should paint a picture of failure, loss (time and money), inefficiency, wastage, and laboriousness. We need to form an image in the buyer's mind of a Groundhog Day situation, where they make poor decisions about their next step and choice of provider, causing them to end up at square one several months or years later.

The shame.

The damage to reputation.

The losses that mean they're actually further back than square one because the time and money they've wasted will never be recovered.

Your invalidation statements should culminate in a message that convinces your buyer that they are highly likely to experience that setback unless they choose your solution, which is guaranteed to help them avoid that "square one" scenario altogether.

What does a differentiated experience look and feel like?

Another way to find the "friction" is to ask customers and prospects about their experience of working with competing solutions providers. This will identify the "hoops" that their clients are made to jump through. What can you add or remove? How can you design and sell a more perfect, friction-less experience?

First, imagine you have two buyers. We'll call them Janet and James. Janet will be buying from you; James will be buying from one of your direct competitors (foolish James).

Question #1

During the buyer journey, what does James have to do that Janet doesn't?

In other words, what action can we remove from our buyer journey to make it simpler and less time-consuming for the buyer?

Question #2

Why does Janet feel that this solution is better suited to her and the needs of her company than James does?

Here, we're looking at how tailored the solution is and how well-positioned your offering is, to solve the specific challenges in front of it. Perhaps your competitor offers a solution that covers many sectors and buyer types whereas yours is hyper-targeted to the pains and frailties suffered by your niche or chosen segment.

Question #3

What does James have to wait for that Janet does not?

The three main considerations any buyer has are time, quality and price. The old adage states that you can only have two of them: that something of high quality and low price will take time and effort to create and deliver; that you'll have to sacrifice quality if you require something fast and at low cost. You get the idea.

With Question 3 we want to uncover the inefficiencies in the competing proposition. What does James have to wait for with the alternative supplier to generate the results he desires?

By identifying these inefficiencies, you'll uncover opportunities to dial up your own offering by removing some of the superfluous delays and other sacrifices the buyer must make. This will generate the superior experience you're striving for.

Above are just three example questions we use to identify friction points for positioning against. We have dozens in our locker. Reach out if you'd like more ideas.

CLIENT STORY – The Project Foundry

A rapidly growing professional services firm based in Dublin, Ireland, The Project Foundry was positioned as (yet another) digital transformation specialist before working with us. Their growth demonstrated a wealth of sales success and their record of retention and repeat business cemented the belief that they needed little help in sales and marketing.

Their sector is rife with "body shops" – companies that recruit workers to fulfil the needs of their clients on a short-term contract basis. Also, the "Big Four" consultancies were looming with competitive bids for work. The leadership was well-versed in the statistics on projects delivered by particular "top tier" consulting giants and these statistics didn't make for comfortable reading!

The leadership team within The Project Foundry saw their position in the marketplace as MEH and needing a lift. They wanted to become less reliant on referral and word-of-mouth business while adding a "net new" arm of marketing-sourced opportunities to fuel further explosive growth. During the invalidation phase, some true gems emerged – highlighting why competitors were inferior not only in how they presented their solutions but also in the delivery of the work.

Armed with this insight on competitors, identifying friction, invalidating competing solutions and creating compelling alternatives became far more straightforward. The Project Foundry used our workshop to cement its vision and mission and continue to use the tools to work through value propositions. They're building upon their successes and are now equipped with a unified, attention-earning voice to match their ambitions.

A Different Result

At various points in this book, I have to defer to some well-known quotes and platitudes. Forgive the MEH.

Those in business will no doubt be familiar with the phrase "People aren't interested in you but in what you can do for them". It's true. In fact, it's a human condition. Even the most philanthropic and charitable acts are often motivated by a personal sense of achievement and a general desire to feel better about ourselves.

And so it is in the world of B2B marketing. Many moons ago, I travelled to the Business Networking International (BNI) conference. BNI is a global business network with enough chapters (local groups) to rival the Hells Angels but with a heavier emphasis on referrals and full English breakfasts than on motorbikes and road trips!

One of the headliners at the conference was Andy Bounds, speaker and author of "The Jelly Effect", in which he talks about the importance of effective communication and how to achieve it.

One thing that Andy spoke about, which has stuck with me more than a decade later, is the seemingly contagious issue of companies talking about themselves on their websites and in marketing materials. He suggested a simple exercise: print off your company website and use two highlighter pens of differing colours (let's say red and blue).

Next, highlight any copy (text) that speaks about your company in red and that speaks about your clients and their challenges in blue.

The result? If it's more red than blue, you lose.

Take a look at your website and those of others in your category. My guess is that you'll find plenty of statements and headlines that begin "We are…" or "We do…" or "We help…". Andy calls this "We'ing over your prospects".

It's a problem.

Why is it a problem?

Because your buyers are experiencing pains and problems every day. They're frustrated. They often feel pangs of guilt and imposter syndrome at not being able to fix the situation. They may have tried various solutions already, to no avail, which only goes to exacerbate the problem and their heightened sense of failure.

Your buyers want the solution. They want to hear about the nirvana-like existence that they can experience on the "other side" of the challenge. At this stage, they're more interested in how your solution differs from their failed attempts of the past than how many years you've been in business or what awards you've picked up along the way.

I'm not suggesting that "social proof" and credibility is not essential to your ability to close the deal. But at the point of initial attention and connection, your buyers will be looking for the fix and how it can uniquely help them.

What does your buyer want to "receive" more than anything?

I've spent the vast majority of my working life selling services and, with that, comes a mighty challenge: selling intangibles.

By default, buyers like to "touch and try" before purchasing. It's the reason why any SaaS business worth its salt leads with a free trial or demo of the product. It provides potential buyers with the confidence that they're making an informed and considered decision based on experience.

In the services business, nobody can take your solution down from a shelf, turn it around in their hands or give it a squeeze to assess its quality. As much as solutions providers try to package up their services and "productise" them the best they can, they're still "selling air". Whilst the results may be seen and experienced down the road, there's nothing to see or feel at the point of sale.

But the buyer still wants the outcome. The result. Something that helps them feel confident in their decision and avoids the feeling that they're simply repeating their mistaken choices of the past.

That fear is very real. I've experienced it many times in marketing and I'm guessing that many of you reading this will have had a poor experience with a marketing agency or "expert". Perhaps the promises were grand but the results were far from it. Perhaps, even, (and I've heard this more times than I can really believe) you forked out a great deal of cash only to receive no value or outcome whatsoever.

These stories and experiences often elevated the sense of fear and reluctance in our prospects. As much as they saw the logic in our proposal, they found it difficult to get over the pain of the past. In effect, our sales conversations started many yards before the start line and we found ourselves having to make up that lost ground before we could discuss any meaningful engagement.

So, how do we overcome the "intangible factor" or lessen the impact of past failures on the buyer's ability to make a purchase decision?

The quantifiable result

The quantifiable result is a timely outcome that you can deliver to any client to deflate the sense of commitment in the deal, increase confidence EARLY in the engagement and ultimately set the tone for a successful working relationship for as long as you choose to maintain one.

It can be an instance of social proof – a particularly impressive result that you generated for a client. I'm a big fan of the concept "once is fact". You promote a result you generated, as a present-tense outcome that you offer to prospects, based on the fact that you've proven you can do it.

It's *not* a promise that you will achieve that specific outcome for that prospect because that will depend on the needs of the particular prospect. You could fall short or produce an even better result for them!

Regardless, the purpose of the quantifiable result, positioned as a prior win, is to suggest an outcome that's relevant and compelling enough to earn the attention of more like-minded buyers and get into conversations with them.

Your quantifiable result may not be from a social proof "win" but a tangible deliverable placed in the hands of the client in the early stages of the relationship, and which delivers huge value.

It can be a stepping stone to the longer-term project or deliverable. Perhaps it relates to the first step of your Unique Mechanism. A common deliverable in the initial phase of a B2B engagement is a documented strategy or roadmap. This might result from a paid or unpaid discovery phase or workshop, designed to add clarity to the terms of the engagement whilst also being inherently useful and enlightening.

Which is better, *quantifiable* or *tangible*?

In my experience, and after much testing in the field, a quantifiable result trumps a tangible outcome for grabbing attention. Does that contradict my earlier comments about people's love of tangibility? Not exactly. You see, before you decide to take anything down from a shelf and give it the once-over, it first has to earn your attention.

Numbers earn attention like very few things, especially in business and especially if the outcome that's most desired by your buyers is tied to a prevalent metric or KPI.

365% ROI.

3× win rate.

Triple your revenue.

137 man-hours saved.

These are all examples of quantifiable results. Perhaps similar claims have grabbed your attention in the past? As you consider the above examples, I'm guessing you're already forming judgments about their legitimacy or accuracy.

And that's exactly what your buyers will do, too.

There are three aspects that we'll need to account for, each triggering thoughts and feelings in the recipient:

1. **Believability**

   Is the claim so outlandish as to be unbelievable or unattainable to the prospect?

2. **Relevance**

   Is the result likely to be attainable relative to this specific prospect's situation? This is where segmentation helps.

3. **Excitability**

   Is the claim compelling and attractive enough to get the prospect excited? A 365 percent ROI might be exciting enough but a 2 percent return on investment? Not so much!

There's another factor that I hope should be obvious but probably bears mentioning...

Authenticity.

The claims you make should be legitimate and honest. Whilst your quantifiable result should be attention-grabbing, you should be able to explain in greater detail with the facts of how that result was achieved (if that's your chosen format) or will be achieved once the deal has been agreed.

If need be, apply caveats and conditions on the outputs of the process. If the outcome is likely to be starkly different from the one cited, be up-front and honest about that. If the result is in any way dependent on the client fulfilling certain obligations or on third-party factors outside of your control, make these elements obvious before moving forward.

With great power (the ability to MEHscape) comes great responsibility. Anyone can inject excitement and intrigue into their positioning with lies but your reputation and existence as a business will be under considerable threat if you do.

What's so MEH about your current offering?

Is it possible that you're already promoting a quantifiable result that's good enough to earn and retain the attention of your ideal buyers?

Of course it is.

But it's unlikely. And here's why...

In my experience, B2B company leaders are reluctant to sing their biggest wins from the rooftop of business. Whilst there's a never-ending effort to capture and publish case studies and testimonials, there never seems to be enough of this social proof available.

When the social proof is readily available, the examples used often fail to fully reflect the sorts of buyers that you wish to attract more of. It's not just industry sector relevance that counts but also other factors like location (market) and size of company. Many companies have case studies representing smaller clients than they wish to entice in the future but the reverse is also true.

A client we worked with in early 2022 had a wealth of examples of household name brands, whose fortunes they had positively impacted. But their latest proposition was aimed squarely at small-to-medium sized companies.

As we touched on earlier, whilst the logos of Samsung, O2 and Honda might appear impressive to most, they may strike fear into the smaller business owner or leader. For instance, they may suggest that the solution is going to be too expensive.

Perceived "heavyweight" credibility is not *always* a good thing! It's far more important to match the pace and ambitions of those you're trying to attract.

If the result you're currently offering is not rooted in social proof and your best past win, and is more aligned with a tangible "stepping stone" deliverable or outcome that is not producing the desired effect, perhaps it could benefit from some of the MEHscapology treatment. The deliverable itself may need an identity or some new language to make it "pop" and pique the necessary levels of intrigue.

Revisit the "Different Language" section and adopt the same process to add that vital X factor to your offer.

Why is a quantifiable result so important?

The absence of an outcome plays on the buyer's mind and creates doubts:

- Doubt that they will receive value early on in the engagement
- Doubt that there's any accountability for results
- Doubt that the solution is any different than the others they've tried or disqualified in the past

Whilst these doubts persist, it leaves reason and opportunity for your prospect to exit the discussion and never darken your door again. The presence of doubt equates to the looming possibility of "No".

A viable quantifiable result will achieve one of two things:

- Amplify or improve a particular metric
- Remove or decrease inefficiencies

Providing an attractive ROI, increasing profitability, growing the pipeline and improving the win rate are all examples of outcomes that improve or amplify.

Saving man hours, cutting processing time, removing costs and identifying wastage are all examples of reducing or removing inefficiencies.

It's highly likely that your solution or solutions provide multiple benefits, milestones and deliverables that fit in both columns. Shortly, I'll show you how to identify them, before distilling them down to the most compelling option to weave into your positioning.

Time to deliver

Another variable must be attached to your quantifiable result to maximise its impact: time.

There's a limited window in which your buyer will need to see a tangible or metrics-based outcome before they feel uncomfortable and unwilling to engage at the highest level. It's best to communicate this at the earliest possible stage to remove all doubt in the "buyer brain"...

90 days.

I'll admit there's no hard and fast rule around this and I can only speak from vast experience.

When we've tested these propositions and messages with target buyers across a range of B2B business models, sectors and buyer profiles, we've found the ideal timescale for delivery of your result, interim or otherwise, is 90 days.

Anything more feels like a huge commitment and difficult to fathom.

How do you eat an elephant?

One bite at a time.

With very few exceptions, the clients I work with generally seek a long-term, multi-year working relationship with their clients. Monthly (if not annual) recurring revenue reigns supreme and makes for stability and predictability in the business from a financial standpoint. It also means a high lifetime value for deals.

But presenting a proposal to a client for a five-year engagement is likely to invoke some nervous twitches, foot shuffling, and a long sales cycles and decision-making process.

This is where a quantifiable result, delivered *inside* 90 days, comes in very handy indeed.

I say *inside* 90 days because your promised outcome could arrive in six weeks, 30 days, 14 days or even a week or less.

As with many aspects of your offer, you need to strike a balance. The outcome needs to be of sufficient perceived value but not take so long to deliver that it reeks of excessive commitment.

And if you cannot fathom a result that you can deliver in such a short timeframe, it likely needs some further exploration. Ask me for some advice and I'll be only too happy to generate some ideas with you.

How to identify your best quantifiable result

Let's take a look at my process for identifying and capturing your quantifiable result, before considering a "pro tip" for boosting its impact:

Step 1 – Dig out your best case studies and testimonials. Bring together the results you've generated in the business to date. Pay particular attention to outcomes delivered for clients you enjoyed working with and want to attract more of due to high enjoyability, fit, profitability, quality of work, etc.).

Step 2 – Bring together your team players responsible for generating results for your clients. In the absence of documented outcomes and social proof, these key people can help you to identify the outcomes you should be attaching your success to. This could include key account managers, client success reps, consultants and may be the same "brain trust" people you assembled for the Discovery stage (segment, persona and challenge).

Step 3 – Using the input of your evidence (social proof) and feedback from the team, create an exhaustive list of the numbers-based results and tangible deliverables you've provided to your best clients.

Step 4 – Take a look back at your Unique Mechanism and consider delivering a subset of the overall process – for example, step one alone. Is there a deliverable or result associated with the completion of that step that you could deliver within the 90-day timeframe? For example, if step one is a workshop or paid discovery meeting, is there a report, roadmap or strategy that you deliver in document (tangible) form?

Step 5 – Note how long it took you to achieve that result from start to finish and make a side note of any determining factors or conditions that would need to be met to achieve similar results again. If you're nervous about the timescales and the possibility of setting unrealistic expectations, err on the side of caution and suggest a longer time period (but keep it within 90 days).

You have your list. Now let's distil it down to the most impactful result or outcome as it appears to your prospective buyer. If you still have your brain trust assembled, there may be some strong opinions about which option is not only most appealing to your buyer but which you have the most confidence in delivering.

At this stage, you may have identified or created a new deliverable never before seen in your business. More than a few of our clients have completed this process, only to craft a completely new-to-market deliverable that offers oodles of value to the client and injects a huge differentiating factor into an increasingly MEH-resistant proposition.

Pro tip

If you went through your list of achievements and deliverables, completed the distillation process and were left disappointed to leave one or more killer outcomes on the table, completely unused, then here's the good news.

You don't have to stick with just one!

The successful delivery of solutions is often achieved through the delivery of several key outcomes over time. Yes, you may deliver a workshop and roadmap in the first 14 days but within 60 days of that, you've also implemented the first major recommendation from that plan.

This is where "result stacking" comes in.

The promise of one milestone being achieved, followed by one or more others, all inside the first 90 days of the engagement will, in most cases, amplify the impact of your offer. It will cement the thought in your buyer's brain that you're backing yourselves to deliver huge value, fast.

And when buyers do receive the benefit of those stacked outcomes, they can get really excited about the longer-term relationship, safe in the knowledge that they've engaged with a firm that does what they say they will do, are trustworthy and credible and, basically, just get sh*t done!

As a defined, modular, ring-fenced deliverable, your quantifiable result can be the focus of any guarantee or de-risking strategy you adopt in your positioning, too. More on that, later.

Finally, consider that an uber-attractive quantifiable result that's packed full of value and significance to your buyer can effectively become what you're known for, as a business. Countless companies only ever promote their leading "foot in the door" solution. The only "promotion" that happens thereafter is discussions with existing clients about the suite of other solutions, services and benefits you can bring to them.

Selling to existing clients is easy; when the upsell/cross-sell comes immediately after you've just delivered a result that moves them giant steps forward.

Got your quantifiable result? Is it impactful and attractive enough to convince your buyers that they're about to experience "Christmas morning" in working with you?

Great! Before we move to the final barrier-breaker to your offer, let's look at how a qualitfiable result helped another client.

CLIENT STORY – NextWave

NextWave provides expert consultancy to clients in the financial sector, with particular expertise in the field of digital transformation. As with the majority of companies that I work with, it's a ruthlessly competitive space and one that's wracked with "sameism". In fact, I would say that there are very few phrases in use today in the B2B space that are uttered more frequently than "digital transformation". It's up there with "cybersecurity" as one of the most overused terms.

We worked through every facet of the MEHscapology process with NextWave but it was in the determination of a quantifiable result that brought the real breakthrough. The company had a full suite of deliverables and promises that they could extend to prospective clients, though they weren't leading with any of them. Like most, they adopted a conservative stance rather than making what they perceived to be bold claims.

Once we'd nailed NextWave's category ownership – claiming their place as specialists in "digital acceleration" – we were able to distil down the quantifiable result options to those related to automation efficiency. This included reducing the time required for vital data processing from four weeks or more to just five minutes! We brought the options down to a tight shortlist, each of which could be delivered to the client within 90 days of deployment.

The result is a pitch that delivers an attractive promise that, once seen, cannot be unseen, and delivers the attention and engagement that NextWave can turn into real business.

A Different Risk

Put yourself on the buyer's side for a few moments. Yes, we've been talking about how to position your solutions and services but at some point – likely recently – you've been the buyer. You may have been the prospect in the sales process for a complex solution that you felt would move your business forward.

Maybe it was marketing services, an IT supplier or business coach/consultant. Whatever the solution, there's likely a point in that purchase journey at which you visualised a scenario of complete failure in the engagement.

If it was marketing, you may have envisaged paying the retainer for several months only to see no increase in traffic, leads or opportunities in your pipeline. For IT services, perhaps you pictured a technical solution being deployed at great cost, only for hackers to gain access to your most confidential client data. Perhaps the business coach would give you advice that results in no growth whatsoever and you find yourself spinning your wheels for several months before parting ways.

Where did these doubts come from?

It may have been an absence of some factors we've discussed in this book so far: no unique and proven mechanism for delivery, no quantifiable result or an overly generic offer suggesting that the supplier didn't really understand you or your industry.

The doubt could also arise from poor past experiences. No matter how different the option in front of us appears and sounds, we just can't shake the failures and bad choices of the past or the associated pains and shudders of the whole galling experience.

Fool me once, shame on you. Fool me twice, shame on me!

It's a natural response but, stepping back into the "seller" role once more, it's one that we must account for and obliterate to guarantee the deal.

Guarantee reluctance

There's a widespread reluctance to provide guarantees across the B2B landscape. If you're willing to step outside your comfort zone, you'll find a real opportunity to be in the minority. See, even within the context of your un-turn-downable offer, we're still taking steps to fuel your differentiation efforts, too.

Let's explore the reluctance with guarantees, as there's every chance that you too are suffering some "head trash" around this subject.

"What if they demand a refund after we've invested all this time, resources and effort into the project?"

"The results will be different for every client we work with, so how can we possibly define a guaranteed outcome?"

"What if we deliver bags of value and the client still challenges the minutiae of the guarantee to find some sort of loophole?"

And the ultimate head trash...

"What if we simply fail to deliver a result?"

Does the reluctance indicate an element of imposter syndrome or doubt in your own solution? Not always but even the most battle-hardened business leader can suffer pangs of doubt in their skills and abilities, especially in bespoke engagements that don't conform to a templated approach.

Some solutions operate under so many variables that you can never really predict, let alone guarantee, a certain outcome.

I've seen it in "marketing agency land", time and time again. The absence of guarantees creates a deafening silence in an industry where so many companies have "had their fingers burned". The promises and expectations are often ramped up sky high and the results generated are subsequently valley-low.

Prospects who have experienced the lows of working with less-than-competent marketing agencies will ask for guarantees, results-based deals and anything that provides some confidence that failure won't see them out of pocket.

But that doesn't account for lost time – the only thing that, once spent, you can never get back. How does any guarantee or risk removal strategy account for, and compensate for, lost time?

Why remove risk?

From your own experiences, you should be able to understand that there's always an element of doubt in buyers' minds that the engagement will fail to deliver what they need.

Accordingly, B2B purchases are typically now decided upon by committee. There may be 12 or more people involved, comprising researchers, ultimate decision makers, financial controllers, users, advocates, detractors, etc. That's a lot of voices to hear and concerns to address, and varying degrees of willingness and enthusiasm to account for.

That's why so many in B2B marketing and sales now adopt an ABM (account-based marketing) approach to new business, engaging with as many committee members as possible, spreading influence and a sense of connection and trust between all parties.

Often, the committee-based decision model is adopted by businesses out of fear that any one decision-maker falls foul of making a selection that ultimately falls flat on its face. Whilst some doubt may remain with a committee, the blame can be shared equally. There's no "fall guy".

But, thankfully, the blame game will be avoided with your solution. Understandable fears may be rooted in the failures of the past (other suppliers, specialists and so-called gurus) but there's no evidence to support the fear that you won't deliver what's promised.

Risk is perceived.

The buyer has conjured an image of failure or loss. It's a story that they've told themselves to avoid making a decision that could harm their reputation and credibility, perhaps even their career path and earning potential.

But just as risk is a story told, so too is risk-removal. The reduction or absence of risk can be perceived and that's what we need to spark in our buyers, through our positioning and the offer we present. We must again use language that re-paints the picture to portray future success rather than failure.

This starts with backing yourself to deliver. Frame yourself and your business as the epitome of confidence and assuredness in your abilities and reputation. That's the power of a great guarantee or risk-removal mechanism.

And, much like great positioning as a whole, risk-removal can compound and serve you throughout the client acquisition journey.

It works in the sales process, of course, by removing any lasting objections and reducing friction at the deal close. But it can also make the difference between converting eyeballs to clicks (to use a digital example) and getting casually scrolled past like you're not even there.

You see, at the top of the funnel, when you're generating awareness and reach for your brand, risk removal can help you to stand out and earn that oh-so-scarce attention.

This works especially well if reluctance remains across your traditional (old language) category. The presence of a guarantee, for example, in a sector where they're just not offered, can in itself be a huge differentiator and help you to stand out in the "guarantee graveyard".

What to guarantee

Oftentimes a company's reluctance to offer risk removal is rooted in confusion about what exactly they should guarantee. Many will default to considering the whole engagement or project completion, which is a daunting prospect. Maybe there's a milestone or subset deliverable that could feature in your guarantee instead?

This is where your quantifiable result again becomes useful. It's the perfect object of your risk-removing intentions.

Assuming you didn't skip that part, your quantifiable result is already a well-formed entity. You know its definitions and conditions and if you stick to the rules, it can be delivered within the first 90 days of the engagement.

The perceived risk in any deal tends to be front-loaded and is essentially "disguised mistrust". You haven't yet earned enough credibility in the buyer's eyes. The quantifiable result is your opportunity to build that trust, removing the necessity for guarantees with subsequent phases of work. You're effectively guaranteeing or removing the risk from your "foot in the door" offer or initial deliverable.

This will remove any long-term perceived "on the hook" risks from the commercial relationship. By the time you get there, you'll have demonstrated your worthiness and expertise, sufficient that any talk of risk is long gone.

Types of risk-removal strategies

Let's explore the ways in which you can remove the perception of risk in any deal. It will come as no surprise that there are many different models and types of guarantee but there are a handful that best suit the B2B solutions-based model. You can deploy them with confidence.

Some require more paperwork and effort than others. A few require measurement, reporting and tracking – lots of accountability that you may discard, narrowing the options further.

Let's explore seven options in more detail. Consider which one(s) will best fit your ambitions:

1. Unconditional guarantee

Possibly the scariest of the lot. It won't suit every business model or proposition. This one is a satisfaction guarantee, so consider this: how many of your recent (and not so recent) engagements have resulted in satisfied clients? How likely is it that, in the delivery of your promised quantifiable result, you might cause someone to feel dissatisfied in any way?

The unconditional guarantee is clean and simple – the simplest form of risk removal by far. It tells the prospect that control is firmly with them, whilst conveying a sense of your ultimate confidence in your skills and ability to deliver.

As the name would suggest, you don't get to apply any conditions or caveats to this promise. Everything has to run smoothly and I would suggest that you don't opt for this format of risk removal if any element of a successful outcome is dependent on the client. After all, with no conditions in play, how will you hold them accountable to play their part?

Pros...
- Simple, clean and easy to implement.
- Conveys the ultimate level of confidence in delivery.

Cons...
- Relinquishes control to the client.
- Can be difficult to quantify "satisfaction" – lots of "wiggle room".
- Not suitable if any aspect of success is reliant on the client.

2. Conditional guarantee

This is likely to be the most popular option.

A conditional guarantee allows you to remove or reduce the perception of risk, whilst placing caveats and conditions on the terms of the guarantee to protect both parties. Crafted the right way, it can ensure that your buyer feels assured in their decision to work with you whilst exposing yourself to zero risk, commercially.

The conditions themselves are usually related to the requirements placed upon the client (the provision of certain information and access to certain assets, tools, and resources within certain timeframes), to allow you to meet your obligations and deliver the quantifiable result.

If you're at all nervous at the thought of providing a guarantee, I'd highly recommend you try building out a conditional guarantee to start with.

Pros...

- Provides the necessary level of perceived risk-removal, whilst removing any potential commercial exposure for you.
- Holds the client accountable to deliver required inputs and fulfil their obligations.

Cons...

- Too many conditions and you may destroy the perception of risk-removal altogether – introducing too much "friction" into the agreement.

3. The "more than your investment back" guarantee

This is a bold option. You may have seen it in the form of a "double your money back" guarantee or similar. It's an uber-confident, amplified effort to convey unwavering confidence in your solution.

This form of risk-removal is considered superfluous in most instances but it does have a place with certain propositions. As mentioned earlier, where efforts have failed, it's common for a guarantee to cover the financial outlay but that doesn't account for the lost time – something the client is not going to get back.

Let's assume your guaranteed quantifiable takes 90 days. By the time you've onboarded, delivered, evaluated and presented outcomes, it could easily be four to six months before failure is confirmed and any refund is affected.

The client, too, is still suffering the challenge and now in need of another solution provider, which could take months to properly evaluate and engage.

A "more than your investment back" guarantee could partially compensate for the time lost. It conveys your appreciation for the risk not only of financial loss but time wasting and the "back to square one" scenario that would ensue from failure.

This option may not be very attractive but it remains in the mix for those confident enough to deploy it properly and whose control over the success of the model is assured.

Pros...

- Creates a hugely elevated sense of confidence in your ability to deliver. The ultimate backing.

Cons...

- In extreme circumstances and where there is a legitimate chance of failure, the subsequent costs could be hard to swallow.

4. Performance or results-based charging

This is the one that many marketing agencies avoid like the plague, for fear that their inability to deliver results is exposed!

OK, so that's a tad harsh but I'm actually referring less to the availability of credible marketing agencies (of which there are plenty) and more to expectation-setting and the definition of a "result".

The model of this guarantee is simple. You agree in advance with the client that they will pay you a certain amount to achieve a certain result (after that result arrives). The result will be of sufficient value that a return on their investment is built in and the fee of sufficient value to make it attractive to you.

However, because in this model you assume 100 percent of the risk, the fee usually includes a premium on what could usually be charged in a traditional, non-guaranteed commercial deal. It's "danger money" for assuming the additional risk.

Pros...

- Ultimately attractive to the buyer, who assumes no initial outlay and only pays after you deliver a defined and inherently valuable result.

- Conveys the ultimate confidence in your ability to deliver – the greatest credibility-builder of all the risk-removal options.

Cons...

- You assume all the risk as the provider and only get paid when the outcome is achieved

5. Share of upside

We're getting into "heavy maintenance" territory now, with the sorts of deals that require a LOT of trust and bags of openness. This mode of risk-removal will not be suitable for the vast majority of deals, as it relies on the right business models and outcomes to drive real revenue growth.

Share of upside sees you, as the solution provider, realise a share of the financial gain made as a result of your plan being implemented. It requires deep and accurate attribution – the ability to prove without doubt that your efforts have directly contributed to the commercial upside – and the willingness of the client to open up the books to reveal the "before, during and after" financial situation in the company.

This strategy does, however, ringfence any gains, meaning that no growth (no win) means no payment. In that respect, it may be attractive to some clients, provided they're the sharing type and don't mind a bit of bureaucracy.

If this is a model that you choose to explore, it's best to seek legal advice beforehand to ensure that all agreements are binding and that obligations to share the necessary information are upheld.

Pros...
- Attractive to some buyers, as it restricts any fee structure to the upside gained. No win, no fee.
- For those who provide solutions that result in legitimate financial gains to their clients, this can bring unbridled financial gain throughout the course of the engagement, which often greatly outweighs a traditional fee structure.

- Due to the perceived complexity, this model can be used as a secondary offer that makes a traditional engagement more attractive by comparison.

Cons...

- Lots of paperwork and potential legal contracts to ensure that everyone is protected.
- Won't suit the vast majority of business models and outcomes.
- May be viewed as overly complicated.

6. **Fixed-cost delivery
(work for free until it's achieved)**

Easy to implement and low risk to the seller (without compromising on appeal to the buyer), this is one of my favourites when positioned correctly.

This strategy essentially tells the buyer that you will continue to work to deliver the agreed outcome or quantifiable result, at no additional cost, should delays take you beyond the agreed target date.

It does have potential perceived negative baggage, of course, as it seeds the idea that you won't deliver on time. But, on the plus side, it demonstrates to the buyer that you're committed to delivering the result, come what may, and that your commercial agreement remains unchanged.

An example of this might be "We'll deliver your documented programme recovery strategy inside 60 days or we'll work for free until it's done". If, as in many cases, this is a lead-in to further solutions and services for the long term, this approach can work even better. After all, you're incentivised to complete the initial milestone on time, as it will kick off the subsequent work with the client.

Pros...

- No risk beyond staff costs to deliver beyond any agreed deadline.

- Can be coupled with a conditional guarantee to ensure that any vital client obligations are met as part of the deal.

- Easy to agree and implement – very little complexity.

Cons...

- Could be perceived the wrong way and seed the idea of delays when, in reality, they are unlikely to occur.

7. Reverse guarantee

This is the last example – and a tricky one to pull off. A reverse guarantee is, in reality, the absence of a guarantee. It tells the buyer that all sales are final and that they're on the hook for payment, regardless of the outcome.

Hold on, though. How is this a risk-removal strategy?

Well, as with much of the MEHscapology effort, it's all in the positioning. After all, our job is not to remove or mitigate risk in the deal; it's to remove the *perception* of risk!

The reverse guarantee works well when you have such high value processes and/or tools to provide to the client that once they see or experience it, you've essentially shared with them your intellectual property.

To get this approach to work, you need to convince the buyer that what they will see cannot be unseen and, therefore, a sale is final. Easier said than done!

Pros...

- Removes any risk on the seller's side.

- Can increase the levels of intrigue and excitement in the buyer to new heights.

Cons...

- Can be difficult to craft the right wording to produce the desired perception and result. Could do more harm than good.

Any guarantee or risk-removal strategy is open to scrutiny. It needs to be legitimate, detailed (for the protection of your business as much as the client's), and structured to minimise the likelihood of contention and ill-will, later on.

Nobody wants a refund!

A guarantee or risk-removal strategy is not always about refunds or recovery of investment but for anyone still feeling nervous about guaranteeing their work, this is important...

The client didn't buy from you with aspirations for the project to fail, reclaim their investment and put that money back in their bank account several weeks or months later.

You sold them on the vision of a challenge solved and that's ultimately what they want most. The likelihood of a refund request or invocation of a guarantee is very small, especially where the client has been involved in the process and has witnessed first-hand the time, skills and effort that have gone into the joint endeavour.

At the time of writing, TGO has *never* had a client invoke a refund via our "Lego Fire Walk Guarantee"; a record I'm incredibly proud of and hellbent on continuing. By the way, you can read more about this strangely named guarantee below.

The point is this: when well-crafted, the ultimate risk-removal option won't leave your business exposed to financial loss, which is a primary factor in many people's reticence to offer one. The options and guidance above should help you select the best option for you and your business.

Remember, any reticence that you may feel is shared by others in your sector and, in the search for differentiation, that presents an incredible opportunity.

If you arrive at the conditional guarantee model – ultimately the most popular and mutually protective – here are some tips on how to craft terms that serve both sides sufficiently:

1. **Quantify the risk on both sides**. Sometimes, we have a perception of high risk when, in reality, there is none. Dig into all possible scenarios arising from your work together to see what legitimate downside there is.

   This could include loss of time, revenue, wasted resources or delays to other growth plans and key hires. Be as exhaustive in your exploration as possible.

2. **Identify the variables that influence the certainty of a desired outcome.** Are there elements of the result that rely on the client fulfilling certain duties or delivering certain information or assets?

   List the provision for access to collateral residing with the client. Failure to meet the terms will, of course, render the guarantee null and void.

3. **Consider the timescales** within which the variables must be accounted for to satisfy the term of the deliverable. This becomes especially important if you're guaranteeing the quantifiable result inside 90 days.

   For example, if you offer a workshop and documented roadmap and you know that you need 30 days to compile and document the roadmap, you know that you must have scheduled and completed the workshop at least 30 days before the deadline.

4. **If in doubt, seek legal help** to craft binding conditions that keep everyone protected to the necessary levels.

Presenting your risk removal strategy

When presenting your risk-removal strategy to the buyer, as part of your un-turn-downable offer, you ironically find yourself *at risk* of being a bit MEH! After all, we all encounter guarantees in our daily lives from every direction and related to a wide range of products and services.

To call yours a "satisfaction guarantee" or a "performance-based charging model" would be to fall straight back into the world of tired, old language that lumps us back in with the crowd.

It's time, once again, to reach into the dark recesses of our language-creating minds to concoct some more vocabulary. This time, to describe in vivid, attention-grasping ways how your method eliminates risk from the deal.

This is an opportunity to be playful and it's the stage of the offer that, from experience, is most likely to raise a chuckle from your prospect. And that's a VERY good thing. Laughter invokes a higher level of comfort and implied trust in a potential buyer. In short, if you can make them laugh, you can make them buy!

How do we do it?

By giving an IDENTITY to our guarantee (or chosen strategy) that elevates it above the world of "small print" or legal jargon.

It's difficult to describe without some examples, so here goes...

Here at TGO, we have a guarantee attached to our 'MEHscapology' programme (shameless plug) that is, in effect, a satisfaction guarantee. But we don't label it as such. Instead, we call it our...

Lego Firewalk Guarantee

Let me guess. Your intrigue and curiosity levels have just increased at least a little, boosted by a desire to know what this means, right? That's exactly the goal of this language and positioning.

Under the hood, our guarantee means that if someone completes the differentiation process, takes a look at their newly-rejuvenated positioning and messaging, and wouldn't walk barefoot over loose Lego bricks to keep hold of it, we will refund them in full.

It raises at least a smile every single time we present it. And because this part comes late in the offer, very close to the big "ask" for the business, it's perfectly placed to have the buyer feel good about their decision to proceed.

Now, there's a caveat to all this. The level of fun and humour you can legitimately inject into your guarantee will be determined, at least in part, by the tone you wish to establish and the dynamic between you and your ideal target buyer.

If your company helps people overcome their fear of flying, perhaps a "Fireball death avoidance guarantee" wouldn't be an advisable tone to adopt!

You get the point. Consider your audience and gauge your likely ability to take an off-beat stance whilst maintaining credibility in the deal.

So, that's your action for this section: give YOUR risk removal strategy an identity. Consider the "chuckle factor" and determine how far you can safely go, considering tone and the expectations of your ideal buyer.

Remember, you don't need to go into great detail about the terms and conditions at this point. That comes later. We're still firmly in attention-generating mode and whilst you will need to put everything down in black and white at some point, this stage of the process is simply about removing or dramatically lowering barriers to "Yes".

Get in touch with me about any strategies and identities that you're particularly proud of. I'm always on the hunt for great examples to share with my own audience.

CLIENT STORY – Singularitee

I've worked with a great many managed service providers (MSPs) over the years. It's a highly competitive space, where a lot of the messaging and marketing collateral can innocently be inherited and adopted from the vendors that many MSPs partner with.

Companies like Microsoft, for example, will often "feed" their partners with marketing assets including website copy, email templates, brochures and more. Many partners will use these resources at face value, with no niche application or tailoring in any way.

Singularitee didn't have that problem per se but owner Adam was acutely aware that his website, messaging and overall position largely matched others in the industry. Few differentiating factors were at play in any of their outward communications.

One aspect that stood out in Singularitee's offer was the absence of any form of risk-removal. It's not uncommon for MSP clients to engage them and stay satisfied for many years. In fact, to date, Singularitee have never lost a client in their five or so years of operations. The relationship requires very high levels of trust, as access to client systems and data is afforded to the partnering business.

So, it made sense to introduce some form of guarantee, at least to the point of delivering the agreed quantifiable result. Singularitee's owner-founder, Adam, was struggling for an idea that stood out and demanded attention. When I told him about our own "Lego Fire Walk" guarantee, it suddenly clicked. Adam had himself completed a bona fide firewalk (no Lego, just red-hot coals), so perhaps this could be incorporated into the offer?

The result?

"Adam's Hot Coals Guarantee" which sees Adam retake that feted walk, should Singularitee fail to deliver on their promise.

Rest assured, the terms go far beyond just a night on the coals for Singularitee's esteemed leader, making it a true no-brainer and risk-absent promise.

Bringing it all together

Celebration time! If you made it this far and completed the necessary steps along the way, you now have all the component parts of a highly performant market position and an un-turn-downable offer. You can rightly take your place among the MEHscapee businesses that TGO has helped to claim their "category of one" status, ditch the dull and reap the rewards that come when challenges like same-ism, tumbleweed outreach and MEHssaging are left far behind.

Let's recap exactly what you've done and tick off those component parts:

Discovery done

You've clearly understood that great positioning is highly relevant and targeted in its approach. You no longer speak in generics but have a malleable pitch that can be turned to the specific needs and tone of the ideal buyer who stands before you.

You've captured the key challenges and fears of that buyer. You know their greatest desires and goals for the future. And you understand the obstacles that they feel stand in their way of success. Armed with this information, you've been able to ensure that your core message and offer provides the counterpoint to that pain and suffering they experience, painting a vivid picture of the nirvana-like existence that awaits on the other side of the solution you provide.

Unique Mechanism manufactured

You've now mapped out the proven process for the transformation you deliver. You accept that your buyers need confidence in your process and that a solid roadmap (ideally in a visual format) provides certainty in their minds that they're not a "guinea pig" and that there is structure and consistency in your offer.

You've validated this mechanism, too, by ensuring that the composite stages of the transformation each account for a challenge, a goal or an obstacle and that there are zero superfluous steps addressing no legitimate requirement. In short, your Unique Mechanism delivers on every need with no fluff!

Quantifiable result rendered

You've also articulated the quantifiable result that your buyer can expect, ideally within 90 days of working with you; whether that's a milestone result or metric or perhaps something tangible that can be placed in the buyer's hands. This result may be represented by the completion of one or more stages of your overall mechanism, or (more powerfully) designed to deliver a certain important metric to the client.

You know that this result provides confidence to the buyer that they've made a great decision in working with you and will set the tone for a wonderful longer-term working relationship, if applicable.

Category owned

You should be starting to feel pretty lonely, right about now. That's because you've successfully ejected yourself from that "red ocean" business category that all of your closest competitors inhabit. You've left them to fight for the scraps in that over-crowded market by deploying their generic, cover-all language and propositions.

Instead, you've established your "category of one", and you may have even started to take steps to protect this language via trademarks. One thing's for sure: when you share who you are and what you do with prospects, their interest is piqued and they just HAVE to know more!

Language library listed

That category ownership carries over into your wider language, too. Everything from the challenges you help to solve, the solutions you provide, the people and stakeholders involved on both buyer and seller sides, even down to the marketing assets you deploy. Everything has its own label and an identifier that doesn't make you sound like anyone else.

This new vocabulary ensures that any hard-earned buyer attention is retained throughout the buyer journey and maximises the potential to convert every "great fit" buyer you engage with into new business.

Alternatives invalidated

Even though you now occupy a category of one, you've also found several ways in which to switch the buyer's mind OFF to any competing provider or perceived solution. You recognise that if an alternative path remains viable to your prospective buyer, it could mean a hard "No" to your offer.

Instead, you've closed off those competing avenues and left your solution(s) as the only viable route. Anything else would be patently ridiculous and any legitimate prospect should now feel foolish to turn you down.

Risk removed

Whatever success you've had in achieving the above steps, there may still be a small perception of risk in the deal for your buyer. This is especially true of intangibles: solutions that largely rely on expertise and consultancy. With all the best intentions, quantifiable results, unique mechanisms and such, what if this engagement still fails to deliver the desired result?

That's where your risk-removal strategy comes in. You've now crafted a well-positioned and compelling enough guarantee or similar to fully back yourself. Perhaps you share in the risk that your buyer is taking on or lower the perceived barriers in doing business with you. The result is a complete "no brainer" offer that truly is un-turn-downable!

Position Activation

This is the part where we take the outputs of your positioning and differentiation efforts and put them to very good use, by launching your shiny new offer to an unsuspecting but oh-so-lucky public!

Where do we do this?

Anywhere that your message meets your would-be buyer! That could include your...

- Website
- Email signature
- Social profiles, bio's, headers, etc.
- Pitch deck and other sales collateral
- Print material, business cards and exhibition materials
- Telemarketing scripts, sales scripts and email templates
- Ads and supporting banners/creative
- Audio branding assets, such as podcast and video intros and outros
- Literally ANYWHERE that you intend to source new business from

It's best to prove your offer via a single channel first. Rather than spread yourself thin and dilute the impact of your messaging, we've found it much more effective to throw all your efforts into one channel, such as LinkedIn, to first validate the hard work you've put into your position. Then you can scale your marketing efforts into other areas.

Consistency is key.

At this point, it's worth reminding you to bring your entire team on board first. Achieving a competition-less position is something that needs to be owned by everyone in the business, not just the marketing and sales teams. This will ensure that wherever you're being talked about and whenever your staff are asked "What does your company do?", the answer is uniform and consistent. And, let's face it, many of these conversations will happen outside of professional environments: down the pub, at the school gates, around the Christmas dining table.

The power of those conversations is not to be under-estimated. Everyone is a potential referrer and it's usually the out-of-context, "personal" conversations that spark the greatest opportunities.

Uniformity and consistency should carry over into your professional marketing and sales efforts, too.

Just as your brand guidelines should ensure consistent use of the right fonts, colour schemes and imagery across your marketing arsenal, your "positioning proclamation" should ensure that the messaging, language and supporting calls-to-action are correct and on-point every single time.

How?

You've done the hard work of creating the necessary outputs from this MEHscapology process: from your Unique Mechanism and Quantifiable Result to your Category Ownership and Language Library, as well as your Invalidation Statements and Risk-Removal strategy. These are the building blocks that will help you craft new headlines and messages to deploy in your promotional efforts.

The Next Step

The next step is to create a Client Acquisition Engine that builds upon your differentiated offer and provides a structured, high-converting customer journey.

Your engine incorporates your new language and un-turn-downable offer. It couples this with a marketing strategy that maximises the potential of everything you've created and allows you to run your new business pipeline by the numbers.

When done right, you can effectively reverse-engineer your marketing-sourced sales and revenue goals to "create" success, by knowing the reach and conversion rates required to generate your desired sales results before executing your strategy. When the actual results start coming in, you'll be fully informed about whether it's working, where any bottlenecks exist, and where to focus your "tuning" efforts to break through any dams or blockers that may be hindering the flow of leads through your pipeline.

This is the basis of evidence-based marketing: using factual data to inform what happens next.

The Last Word

Phew! If you've made it here to the end of the book, you've already shown you're more committed than most to finally getting the outcome you want. And if you've done the work I've outlined, you have a business that is set up efficiently and powerfully and ready to bring in a torrent of high-value leads without having to worry about losing them to the competition.

But you might be feeling a bit overwhelmed. And, listen, I get it.

There's a lot to be done. By now, though, you see it's worth it and that not doing the work will cost you far more in wasted time and lost money than you're likely willing to sacrifice. That's the bad news.

The good news is – there's a shortcut...

See, whilst I've shared as much as possible in this book, it would be impossible to share every tool, strategy and exercise that we use at TGO to help companies thrive (fast), by becoming completely differentiated. If I did that, this book would be so thick that no one would ever read it.

With our experience in working with clients just like you and being total nerds for this process, we can do everything outlined in this book (and more!) with or for you – quickly. And that brings me to something very important...

If you ignore what I've shared with you in this book because it seems like "work", please understand that you and your staff will pay the price by having to work harder to generate more leads due to an inefficient business. Your sales team will have to work harder to close sales because your prospects will see you as just one option out of many (rather than the only option). Every part of your business will be tougher than it needs to be. And that robs you of time and energy that could be spent elsewhere.

Whilst I'm a businessman, I'm also a family man. I'm a husband and proud Dad. If my business is exhausting, it takes energy away from me and my family life. If my business is endlessly time-consuming, time is taken away from me. Hobbies and "me-time" also go out the window.

How do I know?

Because that's exactly what happened when I ran an undifferentiated business for so long and just focused on more marketing and more leads.

Those are years I'll never get back.

So, my rally call to you is: please do everything outlined in this book.

Yes, you'll get more business and make more money. But you'll also have more energy and time in your home life. And that's vitally important too. If you know you can and will do this yourself, brilliant! I'm delighted that this book will help you in the way it's intended.

On the other hand, if you have any doubts about whether you can do this yourself or whether you have the time, that's exactly why we exist. There are numerous ways we can help you, at multiple price points, to ensure that this important work does actually get done. Quickly. Don't let this book and the ideas in it just gather dust on your bookshelf whilst you keep swimming against the tide and competing with others. Work with us to ensure your business life becomes far easier and less stressful than it currently is.

To schedule a brief chat with me or a member of my team about our different offerings, please visit **https://matthodkinson.com/ MEHscapology**

Speaking of which, here's one way that you can move your company's positioning and overall marketing forward, without jumping through the usual hoops!

Book a Positioning Pow Wow with me! You'll be prompted to complete our "MEHxamination" quiz to find out how your current positioning and differentiation levels shape up, before we spend a short 15 minutes plotting a course for your category domination. There's NOTHING to buy on the call...

https://matthodkinson.com/MEHxam

Even as I write my very first book, I'm humbled at the thought of a (till now) complete stranger reading this line. I truly hope that even the smallest snippet from these pages has helped to move you towards your loftiest goals and ambitions.

Thank you so much for reading.

Ingram Content Group UK Ltd.
Milton Keynes UK
UKHW032029100423
419806UK00019B/525

9 781399 949699